Horsemen

Blue and Gray

"If you want to smell hell,   *jine the cavalry."*

—SONG OF JEB STUART'S TROOPERS

HORSEMEN

A PICTORIAL HISTORY

BLUE AND GRAY

Pictures by HIRST DILLON MILHOLLEN

Text by JAMES RALPH JOHNSON *and* ALFRED HOYT BILL

New York · OXFORD UNIVERSITY PRESS · 1960

© 1960 BY OXFORD UNIVERSITY PRESS, INC.

LIBRARY OF CONGRESS CATALOGUE CARD NUMBER: 59-10461

PRINTED IN THE UNITED STATES OF AMERICA

Dedicated with respect to the cavalrymen

who have fought in America's wars

Contents

1   *Horsemen Wanted, 3*

2   *Once Around McClellan, 17*

3   *Western Riders, 31*

4   *Jeb Stuart Raids North, 41*

5   *Christmas Behind the Federal Lines, 55*

6   *George Stoneman Raids South, 73*

7   *Near Misses and a Hit, 83*

8   *Morgan Raids North and Quantrill West, 95*

9   *Once Around Rosecrans, 109*

10   *"That Crazy Fool" Kilpatrick and George Custer, 119*

11   *Once Around Lee, 133*

12   *Sheridan's Trevilian Raid, 147*

13   *Wilson and Kautz on Lee's Back, 157*

14   *Sheridan Cleans the Shenandoah, 167*

15   *Hampton's Beefsteaks, 185*

16   *"That Devil Forrest," 195*

17   *The Horsemen in at the Death, 207*

ACKNOWLEDGMENTS, 217
BIBLIOGRAPHY, 221
PICTURE SOURCES, 225
INDEX, 231

Horsemen

Blue and Gray

Lt. Col. George McCabe, 13th Pennsylvania Cavalry, U.S.A.

Capt. James S. West, Confederate Cavalry, C.S.A.

1

Horsemen Wanted

THE AMERICAN CIVIL WAR, which was to
produce such cavalry leaders as Forrest,
Hampton, Kilpatrick, Morgan, Wilson, Sheridan, Buford, and "Jeb" Stuart, began with the
professional estimate of the usefulness of
mounted troops at a low ebb. In the European
armies—notably in the recent Crimean War—
even the usefulness of cavalry for scouting and
screening appeared to have been forgotten. In
the United States mounted troops were regarded as chiefly useful against the Indians on
the western frontier. To be sure, the brilliant
charge of Captain C. A. May's dragoons had
contributed to Zachary Taylor's victory at
Resaca de la Palma in the Mexican War; but
at Buena Vista the magnificent mass attack of
the Mexican lancers had melted away under

THE LAST CHANCE FOR CAVALRY!

FOR THE WAR!

I am authorized to raise a Cavalry company for the war, to
be mustered into Col. Richard Coke's Regiment, in the service
of the Confederate States of America, to consist of one Captain,
one first and two second Lieutenants, four Sergeants, four
Corporals, two Musicians, and not less than 64 nor more than
125 privates.

My commission states that "All parties enlisting in this service will be exempt from draft, and accredited to the respec-
tive counties from which they may come." All officers to be
elected by the company. This is the best chance for immediate service. Each man is required to furnish his own arms
and a good horse.

Texans, your country calls! Come quickly. We will organize as soon as 64 names are enrolled.

JAMES A. THOMPSON.

Austin, Texas, March 16th, 1862.

the fire of Jefferson Davis's riflemen. So when President Lincoln called for 75,000 volunteers in April 1861, it was announced that thirty-nine regiments of infantry would be raised, and only one of cavalry.

Old General Winfield Scott, Conqueror of Mexico and now commander in chief of the Union armies, predicted that the contest would be settled by artillery, and thereafter refused the services of regiment after regiment of mounted troops. The General considered the nature of the American terrain to be unsuitable for the use of cavalry. So the Governor of Illinois wrote in vain to the Secretary of War: "Now Mr. Cameron, please do get General Scott to accept my ten cavalry companies. We

want to be fully ready to take the starch out of the Missouri chivalry." It was not long, of course, before many excellent regiments of cavalry were raised in the Northern states and sent to the front. But for a good while they were used with so little understanding of their capabilities by the army commanders that, "Who ever saw a dead cavalryman?" became a current jibe.

Things were different in the South. However, even there most of the crack militia organizations were battalions of infantry, and the Confederate government refused cavalry companies as late as August 1861. At Richmond, membership in the Fayette Artillery and the Howitzers was as important socially as that in

President Lincoln and General Scott review a regiment of three-year volunteers on Pennsylvania Avenue before the White House.

The newly organized 1st Virginia Cavalry during a halt.

the Henrico Light Dragoons. But up in the Shenandoah Valley, under the stress of actual war, General Joseph Johnston "became more convinced daily of the great value of cavalry compared with infantry, for service on this frontier." He held a meeting of his officers to draft a leader for his mounted troops; and James Ewell Brown Stuart, the "Jeb Stuart" dear to the hearts of all good Southerners, accepted the command.

A born leader and a born cavalryman, Stuart quickly made cavalry out of his collection of enterprising wild horsemen. He soon was able to report that they knew enough to be officers and would soon become good soldiers. As the First Virginia Cavalry, the Inspector General found them "in very good condition, and quite effective. Their arms are a small-sized revolver and a saber . . . The horses are good, and all the men ride well." Though they were hardly the "dashing dragoons" of romance, they were men like those Confederate cavalry of the west, of whom General William Tecumseh Sherman was to report to his War Department: "War

5

U.S. Cavalry Saber, Model 1860. Contract piece imported by Henry Boker for sale to U.S. Government during the Civil War.

U.S. Cavalry (Dragoon) Saber, Model 1840, made by Ames.

Foreign Cavalry Saber. Imported by the U.S. Government during the Civil War.

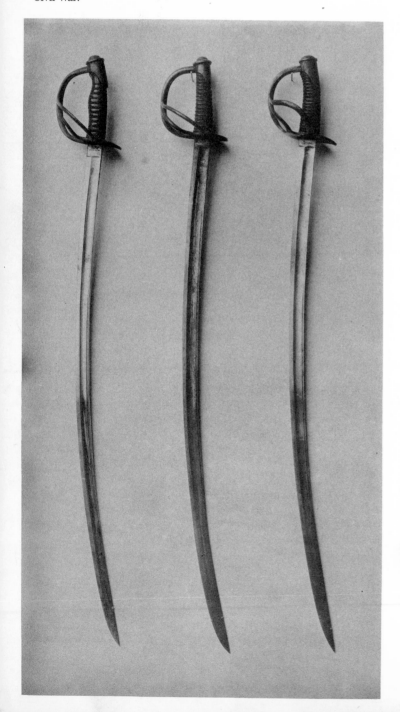

Believed to be a portrait of Turner Ashby as Captain of a troop of cavalry known as Ashby's Mountain Rangers, which he organized before the war.

suits them. The rascals are brave, fine riders, bold to rashness, and dangerous subjects in every sense. They care not for niggers, land or anything. They hate Yankees per se, and don't bother their brains about the past, present, or future."

It proved easy to make cavalrymen of Southern boys from mountains, farms, and wide-open spaces. This fact gave the Confederacy an edge over the North. "The habits of the Southern people," grumbled one Federal general, "facilitated the formation of a cavalry corps . . . comparatively efficient even without instruction." "We were equipped largely at our own and the community's expense," said Captain Charles M. Blackford, Second Virginia Cavalry, "and were armed with double-barrel shotguns, pistols and sabres. It was supposed the shotgun would be an efficient arm, but it

A stockade guards the Washington end of the Long Bridge across the Potomac against raiders.

was too frail and was soon abandoned. After the first battle of Manassas we supplied ourselves with the captured arms of the enemy and had good carbines for the rest of the war." Indeed, in the course of the war the Confederates were to pick up from the battlefield 150,000 of the estimated 400,000 small arms they used. With regard to their troopers' other equipment it should be mentioned that the men generally furnished their own horses and were paid for them only if the animals were killed.

Even before Stuart's arrival, there already existed in the Valley a small organized force of Southern horsemen. This was a company that Turner Ashby, a Virginia planter, had organized back in the fall of 1859 to guard the crossings of the Potomac against any possible repetition of John Brown's raid. It was helping

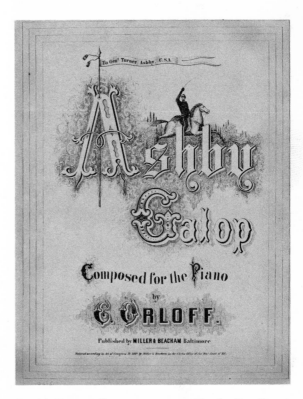

A patriotic songwriter names a composition for Gen. Turner Ashby, c.s.a.—and puns.

to guard the bridge opposite Point of Rocks early in 1861. At Winchester in June of that year it was incorporated in the Seventh Virginia Cavalry and had a part in Stuart's maneuvers that masked Joseph E. Johnston's withdrawal from the Valley to support Beauregard at First Manassas. Ashby became colonel of the regiment that December, and he so skillfully aided General T. J. "Stonewall" Jackson to chase Banks down the Valley the following May that he was made a brigadier general on the 27th. On June 6, however, a Federal bullet brought to a close what promised to be one of the most brilliant careers in the Confederate cavalry.

North of the Potomac, "men accustomed to . . . horses and arms were comparatively few . . . and required training in everything," as Federal instructors found out to their exasperation.

Sgt. Lewis F. Brockman,
Co. M, 2nd Minnesota Cavalry, U.S.A.

Union cavalry on reconnaissance in front of Fairfax Court House.

8

Bull Run: The Confederates' Black Horse Cavalry charge the New York
Fire Zouaves.

Except for the Mid-Westerners, the Union cavalry recruits were generally accustomed to using carriages, buses, or wagons, when they did not walk. Many of them had the effrontery to prefer dark horses to gray, since the grays showed dirt so plainly; and one, an Irishman, sympathetically took the stack of bedding and pots and pans from his overloaded saddle and put them on his own back to relieve his mount of their weight.

At the first major battle of the war—the First Manassas, or, as the Yankees called it Bull Run—the soldiers on both sides learned a great deal "the hard way." "We foresaw the action several days ahead," wrote a Confeder-ate surgeon. "The enemy were known to be advancing in immense masses from Arlington towards Fairfax, and the master stroke was at once made, Johnston down from Winchester, by forced marches [actually by railroad trains] before Patterson could get down the other side."

General Robert Patterson was supposed to contain Johnston in the Valley. But Stuart's cavalry had helped to frighten the old Federal general into the belief that he had to defend himself against an attack by a Confederate force of 35,000; and meanwhile, Johnston and Stonewall Jackson rushed eastward to support Beauregard's left flank at Manassas Junction.

9

10

Col. John E. Wynkoop, 20th Pennsylvania Cavalry, U.S.A., and wife.

Col. Andrew J. Morrison, 3rd New Jersey Cavalry, U.S.A.

Capt. Henry B. Hays, 6th U.S. Cavalry, U.S.A.

Col. Jacob Higgins, 1st Pennsylvania Cavalry, U.S.A.

Lt. Col. Charles E. Capehart, 1st West Virginia Cavalry, U.S.A.

11

Col. James B. Swain, 11th New York Cavalry, U.S.A.

Maj. Anton von Peuchelstein, 4th New York Cavalry, U.S.A.
(*captured at Port Republic, Va., June 9, 1862*)

Col. James H. Childs, 4th Pennsylvania Cavalry, U.S.A.
(*killed in Maryland Campaign*)

Col. Thronton F. Brodhead, 1st Michigan Cavalry, U.S.A.
(*mortally wounded at Manassas, August 30, 1862*)

Stuart led his column in the direction of the firing, and Adjutant W. W. Blackford, who rode at his side, recorded the action: "There right in front, about seventy yards distant, in strong relief against the smoke beyond, stretched a brilliant line of scarlet—a regiment of New York Zouaves in column of fours, marching out of the Sudley road to attack the flank of our line of battle . . . They were all looking toward the battlefield and did not see us."

"I took them to be ours," Jeb laughed later, "and exclaimed with all my might: 'Don't run, boys: we are here.'" Such mistakes of identity were common in those early days of the war when both sides went into battle in fancy-dress uniforms. Then Stuart saw the flag of the United States and ordered the charge, "waving his sabre," Blackford remembered, "for the rear to oblique to the left, on right into line, so as to strike the enemy in echelon, and this they did . . . Half the distance was passed before they saw the avalanche coming upon them, but they came to a front face—a long line of bright muskets was leveled—a sheet of red flame gleamed . . . The smoke that wrapped them from our sight also hid us from them. They lowered their pieces to load, and in this position we struck them."

The charge had taken place so quickly that Blackford did not have time to draw his saber or pistol. He swung his carbine from his shoulder. "I leaned down with my carbine cocked, thumb on hammer and forefinger on trigger, and fixed my eye on a tall fellow . . . rammed the muzzle . . . into the stomach of my man and pulled the trigger . . . he tried to get his bayonet up to meet me; but he was too slow."

When the battle, badly mismanaged on both sides, degenerated into the rout of the Federal army, widespread rumors of pursuing waves of Confederate horsemen accelerated the flight.

Pvt. Jonas Nathan Shuler, Co. E, 10th Illinois Cavalry, U.S.A.

"Blackhorse cavalry" and "masked batteries" had for some time been bugbears among the more imaginative in the Federal army. "'Cavalry are coming!' rang through the crowd," reported a British newsman caught up in the panic, ". . . I perceived coming down the hill . . . a number of mounted men who might at a hasty glance be taken for horsemen in the act of sabering the fugitives . . . They were soldiers and civilians . . . who were whipping and striking their horses with sticks."

Federal officers were disgusted with their own cavalry. Sherman said to the British reporter after the battle: "As to cavalry charges, I wish we had had a few cavalry to have tried one; those Black Horse fellows seemed as if their horses ran away with them."

In the long breathing spell that followed the battle, Stuart's horsemen were employed in

13

Pvt. Alexander Spiers George, Co. F, 10th Virginia Cavalry, c.s.a.

Pvt. Phillip W. Carper, 35th Battalion, Virginia Cavalry, c.s.a.

screening the Confederate army as it lay, almost within striking distance of Washington. Growing throngs of admirers infested their camp. Prince Napoleon, who was making a tour of the United States, was a visitor. "What struck us," noted a member of his party, "was the cavalry . . . Nothing is as picturesque as the Southern cavalry. They wear the most impossible outfits: mostly rags, hats without bottoms, boots without soles. Yet they could make Don Bazan jealous of their martial bearing and countenance."

But there was nothing ragged about Jeb Stuart's appearance, and his frequent cavalry reviews were spectacular. "He had something of Murat's weakness for the vanities of military parade," the Frenchman observed. "He betrayed this latter quality in his jaunty uni-

form, which consisted of a small gray jacket, trousers of the same stuff, and over them high military boots, a yellow silk sash, and a gray slouch hat surmounted by a sweeping black plume." And to these details should have been added the "Jovian beard," which nobody who saw it ever forgot. He saw to it that martial pomp accompanied him wherever he went. A Second Virginia cavalryman wrote of him later in the war: "I was much amused to see Stuart pass through Martinsburg with a large cavalcade of staff and couriers and two bugles blowing most furiously. Lee . . . passed with one or two persons."

In the spring of the next year, 1862, General George B. McClellan, commanding the Federal Army of the Potomac, shifted the war in the eastern theater to Richmond's back door. Soon

Capt. William Wormsley Mead (Loudoun Cavalry), 6th Virginia Cavalry, C.S.A. (Killed at Berry's Ferry, Va., May 16, 1863)

Capt. William E. Rasin, Co. E, 1st Battalion, Maryland Cavalry, C.S.A.

anxious citizens could see the glare of his camp-fires on the evening sky and hear the distant roar of battle in the daytime. Stuart was now a brigadier general and had under him a brigade seasoned by a year of service in combat and skirmish, camp, march, and scouting. They were well armed, with carbine, revolver, and saber. Stuart, like the other cavalry officers who had a West Point training, regarded the saber as the cavalry's weapon for its true function on the battlefield, the charge. The firearms were, of course, the muzzle-loading, percussion-cap weapons of the time, slow to load, especially when the paper cartridges had been softened by dampness or rain. But their large caliber, soft lead bullet had enormous stopping power; and many soldiers liked them so well that they refused to change them for the breach-loaders and magazine rifles that they captured from the enemy in the later years of the war, since the supply of ammunition for the new weapons was bound to be uncertain.

In May of that year, when Stuart's old West Point commandant, Robert E. Lee, took over command of the Army of Northern Virginia from the wounded Joseph Johnston, Stuart was delighted. "We have an army far better adapted to attack than defense," he had the temerity to tell his commander in chief. Lee readily agreed to that. His own choice was always the offensive when he saw better than half a chance of success. The question was where to strike: where was the weakest point in the enemy's line? The north flank, probably. And Stuart was the man to make sure of this.

15

Gen. J. E. B. Stuart, C.S.A.

2

Stuart's saddle.

Once around McClellan

ONE OF THE CHIEF objects of your expedition," Lee told his twenty-nine-year-old cavalry chief, "is to gain intelligence for the guidance of future operations." It was a prudent reminder, for the dashing Stuart throughout his career was all too prone to be carried away by his love of raiding for its own sake. But he "could keep a secret absolutely." During the past winter and spring his officers and men had been able to guess at an impending operation only by observing that "the gayer he was the more likely it was that we were to move soon." Routing out his staff soon after midnight on June 12, he told them: "Gentlemen, in ten minutes every man must be in the saddle."

The guess of the 1200 carefully selected troopers who rode northward from Richmond before daylight that Thursday morning was that they were going to reinforce Stonewall Jackson in the Shenandoah Valley. "Goodbye, boys; we are going to help old Jack drive the Yanks into the Potomac," they told their comrades who were left behind. The force was made up of the First and Ninth Virginia Cavalry regiments, commanded respectively by Lee's nephew Fitzhugh and his second son, William Henry Fitzhugh ("Rooney"); the Fourth Virginia Cavalry; and a detachment of men from the deep South who were drawn from the Jeff Davis Legion and the Boykin Rangers, under the command of Colonel W. T. Martin.

They learned their actual mission "only as the march developed it." The regimental commanders were not briefed until the first bivouac was made, twenty-two miles out on the South Anna River. During the march, scouts had been pushed far out to the right and, after ranging twenty miles southeast that night behind the Federal lines along the Chickahominy, they reported no serious obstacles. At dawn Stuart headed his column in that direction. Fitzhugh Lee's First Virginia swung to one side

17

Pvt. Charles H. Powell, Trumpeter, 4th Virginia Cavalry, c.s.a.

to cut off a Federal force at Hanover Court House, but he ran into a swamp thus giving the enemy time to decamp from what would have been a trap. Bypassing expected contact near Hawe's Machine Shop, Stuart's advance party spotted a line of blue-coated cavalry awaiting them on a slope. But when the Southerners spurted forward in a charge, Federal Lieutenant E. H. Leib ordered a quick retreat. His men's firearms were only pistols and, he explained later: "I felt most seriously the superiority of the enemy, who were armed with rifles and shotguns."

The ruling of the Federal Ordnance Department after Manassas had been that "the orders in the Division of the Potomac are to arm the cavalry with pistols and sabers only." The Department had refused to buy carbines at $35 each, calling the price "too high." As a result the Federal cavalry trooper found his pistol

outranged by the shoulder weapons of Stuart's men. But this preference for the carbine was carried so far by Southern horsemen that, later in the war, many Southern cavalry carried only rifles and no sabers. Confederate General Jubal Early observed that they could not fight on horseback and that in open country they could not fight successfully on foot against large bodies of cavalry.

Stuart pushed on to Totopotomoy Creek, deployed skirmishers to cover his crossing, and drove forward in column of fours. His tactics were "to oppose the enemy with one squadron at a time, a spear to be thrown at any enemy seen." Riding at the head of the leading squadron, Captain William Latane spotted a Federal troop riding from its camp at Old Church to block the road. He led his men against it in a thundering, dust-filled charge that swept it away in a furious hand-to-hand combat. Federal Captain W. B. Royall fell out of the action, "exhausted from loss of blood from several saber wounds." But not before Latane fell with five bullets in his body. "Avenge Latane!" shouted his furious men as they spurred in pursuit.

From prisoners Fitz Lee learned that a detachment of the Fifth U. S. Cavalry, formerly the Second—in which he himself had served— and once commanded by Robert E. Lee, was in front of him. "Burning with impatience to cross sabers with his old regiment," Fitz Lee pushed forward, only to find that his quarry had departed.

Stuart was now faced with the most important decision of the raid. He had secured the desired information: there was little enemy strength along the Chickahominy in the area of Fitz John Porter's corps. He could either retrace his steps or pass through New Kent, which might mean swimming the Chickahominy after making a bold attempt to cut the Federal lines of communication and supply.

The white tents of McClellan's camp at Cumberland Landing were visible for two and a half miles.

"If I returned," he said, "the enemy [would have] had a much shorter distance to pass to intercept me," and since "it was thought probable that the Federal cavalry was concentrating on our rear to cut off our retreat, we kept straight on" toward an unknown reception at Tunstall's Station on the York River Railroad. Closer and on the left was Garlick's Landing on the Pamunkey, a Federal supply base. Five miles east of Tunstall's lay McClellan's White House Landing depot and four miles down the river, the huge Cumberland Landing camp. Some three hundred Federal ships crowded the river between these two points; and what was surmised to be McClellan's headquarters, "surrounded by the white tents of a very large camp, was plainly visible at the distance of two and a half miles."

Gen. Fitzhugh Lee, nephew of Robert E. Lee.

19

Officers of the 5th U.S. Cavalry.

The Jeff Davis Legion, acting as rear-guard, was surprised to be hailed by a group of twenty-five Federal soldiers who, "under the impression that they were surrounded," asked to surrender. Colonel Martin accommodated them. Stuart dispatched a squadron to Garlick's. Soon the startled guard there saw fire sweeping through the rigging of "transport ships . . . laden with wheat, corn, and provisions." Although the actual destruction amounted to only 30 wagons and two schooners, the route began to fill with evidences of hasty flight: "wagons turned over and abandoned—from others the excellent army stores had been hastily thrown . . . other things lay about in tempting array, but we were now approaching Tunstall's," where a moment before a fleeing Federal sentinel had been challenged with "What's to pay?" "Hell's to pay," he had shouted back.

20

Gen. Fitz John Porter, U.S.A.

Stuart's raiders stir things up at Garlick's Landing.

"We marched on briskly," said a Confederate rider, "and arriving near the station, charged down upon it with a yell. We could see the enemy . . . the greater part scattered for cover." Destruction was the order: telegraph poles chopped down; rails torn up; the nearby trestle set on fire. But before this was well under way a train whistle sounded from the west. Obstructions were thrown on the track, and the raiders took cover to fight the Federal reinforcements. It turned out, however, to be a supply train. "The engine driver . . . put on all steam" and knocked the obstructions aside. In vain "a thunderous volley was opened upon the flats" and Stuart's scout Redmond Burke galloped alongside the locomotive in an effort to shoot the engineer. The Federals hugged the floor boards of the cars, and the train rolled on out of sight toward White House.

Riding down to White House, a newspaperman reined in his horse as a "mounted officer dashed past me, shouting some unintelligible tidings, and was followed in quick succession by a dozen cavalrymen who rode as if the foul fiend were at their heels. Then came a teamster, bare-back, whose harness trailed in the road . . . 'The Rebels . . .' he screamed, with white lips." To meet the emergency Lieutenant Colonel Rufus Ingalls, commanding at White House, pulled from their beds 250 hospital patients to reinforce his troops, called up gunboats to cover with their fire the plain over which an attack might come, and sent couriers in all directions for help.

Both the Lees had a strong personal interest in the local situation: "Rooney" Lee owned the historic mansion that gave the place its name. Stuart had an even stronger one: the

21

commander of the Federal cavalry reserve in the area was the frontier soldier, Virginia-born Philip St. George Cooke, who was his father-in-law. Cooke had devised new cavalry tactics for the Federal army, but his son-in-law was putting them in a bad light just now.

The Federal commander, with 500 cavalry, trotted along behind the raiders, collecting infantry with which to block their return. "General Cooke," observed Fitz John Porter, who had little use for Cooke's calculations, "seems to have regarded his force as a reserve. . . . I can only express surprise that General Cooke or General Emory did not join earlier their

Gen. Phillip St. George Cooke, U.S.A.

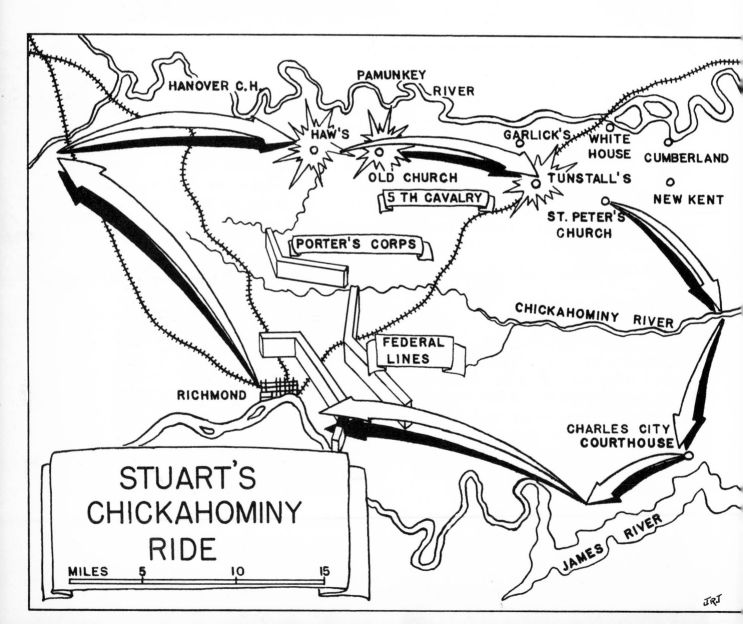

HANOVER C.H.

PAMUNKEY RIVER

HAW'S

GARLICK'S

WHITE HOUSE

CUMBERLAND

OLD CHURCH

TUNSTALL'S

NEW KENT

5 TH CAVALRY

ST. PETER'S CHURCH

PORTER'S CORPS

CHICKAHOMINY RIVER

FEDERAL LINES

RICHMOND

CHARLES CITY COURTHOUSE

STUART'S CHICKAHOMINY RIDE

JAMES RIVER

MILES 5 10 15

The White House was owned by Robert E. Lee's second son, "Rooney."

commands in front . . . and that when General Cooke did pursue he should have tied his legs with the infantry command."

Forgotten Federal units waited patiently for Stuart to come back. Captain Charles Whiting, Fifth U. S. Cavalry, reacted like most of the others: "We reached the crossroad where Captain Royall had been engaged with the enemy about 4:30 P.M., and remained until 3:30 A.M., when we marched to Tunstall's Station . . . and remained until the next morning . . . when we returned to camp."

Stuart, though he admitted to a member of his staff that he "could scarcely resist it," dared not delay his march by an attack on White House Landing. But while he waited anxiously for the detachment sent to Garlick's Landing to catch up with him, he sent his men across the railroad into the "world of wagons loaded with grain and coffee. . . . They were all burned. The roar of soaring flames was like the sound of a forest on fire."

Gen. Rufus Ingalls, U.S.A.

23

White House Landing. Some three hundred Federal ships crowded the river.

As the day darkened into night the tired column turned southward, toward the Chickahominy twelve long miles away. Stuart, "one knee over the pommel of his saddle, folded his arms, dropped the bridle and—chin on breast, his plumed hat drooping over his forehead— was sound asleep," an aide holding his arm to prevent his falling; and whole companies followed the example of their leader until a halt was made below St. Peter's Church.

"The well-filled haversacks with which we started from camp had long since been empty," one trooper remembered. "Fortunately, an enterprising Yankee had established a store here, to catch the trade of all persons passing from McClellan's army . . . He had crackers, cheese, canned fruits, sardines, and many other dainties dear to the cavalryman . . . I fear little was left." Revitalized, troopers who a few hours

before had grumbled, "General Stuart is going to get his command destroyed," now considered him "the first of men."

But the high spirits were short-lived. Dawn showed the raiders stalled by the Chickahominy. "We found the river swollen by recent rains, almost out of its banks and running like a torrent." "Rooney" Lee tested the rapids and came near drowning. "I think we are caught," was his opinion. But Stuart promptly led his column downstream for a mile to where, thirty feet apart, the stone abutments of the destroyed Forge bridge rose above the rushing water. A skiff was discovered and anchored between the abutments as a "movable pier." Boards from a nearby barn formed a footbridge over which the barn timbers could be passed. They spanned the gap, by inches, and floorboards were laid, completing the structure.

24

On June 15, by the James River road, Stuart's command rode back into Richmond. They had ridden around McClellan's whole army, a distance of 150 miles, captured a good many prisoners, and lost but two men: the gallant Captain Latane dead and a trooper missing. They had destroyed enormous quantities of the enemy's supplies and spread confusion through his back areas. Richmond gave them a riotous welcome. Girls strewed flowers before Stuart's horse's hoofs, hung a garland about its neck, and held its rider prisoner until, nothing loath, he declaimed for them his poem, "The Ride around McClellan."

Eleven days later General Robert E. Lee, his army reinforced by the magnificent march of Stonewall Jackson's troops from the Valley, struck where Stuart had revealed McClellan's weakness and began the famous Seven Days Battles. By the end of the next day Fitz John Porter was retreating southward, across the Chickahominy. And once more the Federal cavalry failed to demonstrate their usefulness. According to an observer of one of their attacks, "the butternut infantry" formed "impenetrable squares, hemmed in with rods of steel, and as the enemy horsemen galloped

Stuart's weary men, many asleep in their saddles, halted to rest when they reached St. Peter's Church.

around them, searching for pervious points, they were swept from their saddles with volleys of musketry." Actually the Confederates formed no squares; and the Federal cavalry, badly misused, accomplished little or nothing on these battlefields; though among them were the Sixth Pennsylvania Lancers, who had been called in the Northern papers "the finest body of troops in the world."

"And so they were, so far as their tailors could make them," observed a Confederate.

Lances stacked, men of the 6th Pennsylvania Cavalry (Rush's Lancers) take their ease.

25

"They stood 300 yards from us in line of battle," wrote Stuart's Prussian aide, Heros von Borcke, "and presented . . . a fine martial appearance." W. W. Blackford confessed afterwards: "I felt a little creeping of the flesh when I saw this splendid looking body of men, about seven hundred strong, drawn up in line of battle . . . armed with long poles with glittering steel points. To think of one of these being run through a fellow was not at all pleasant. . . . They lowered their lances to a level and started in fine style to meet us midway, but long before we reached them the gay lancers' hearts failed them and they turned to fly. . . . The road was strewn with lances thrown away. . . . They were certainly well mounted," Blackford added, "[for I] could not overtake them in the mile or two race I gave them, though they had only a hundred yards start."

President Jefferson Davis was not surprised by the victories of the Southern infantry over the Northern cavalry. At Buena Vista he had seen his Mississippians, after a single volley, throw <u>down their</u> rifles, run forward and seize the Mexican lancers' bridles, back the horses on to their haunches, and kill the riders with Bowie knives.

26

Stuart's horsemen, mostly Virginians but already well sprinkled with men from the Carolinas and Georgia, encountered the Federal cavalry a number of times in this Peninsula fighting and "swept them away by the first charge in every case," wrote one of them. "It was a constant regret to us that they would not stand long enough for us to capture their horses and arms, the latter particularly." On the Union side, General W. W. Averell remembered with bitterness the misuse of his command on the Peninsula: "My cavalry was deployed as a close line of skirmishers with drawn sabers in rear of our lines, with orders to permit no one to pass to the rear who could not show blood."

The fighting forced McClellan to shift his base from White House Landing to Harrison's Landing on the James, and the battle of Malvern Hill practically put an end to the Peninsula campaign. In early August President Lincoln ordered it to be abandoned.

Gen. George B. McClellan and his wife.

RIDING A RAID

J. W. RANDOLPH RICHMOND V.ª

LITH BY E. CRE FN

27

RIDING A RAID

Spirited but not too fast

VOICE

PIANO

_mf_   _Cres._

2ᵈ VERSE Now gal_lop now gal_lop to

1ˢᵗ VERSE 'Tis old Stone_wall the Re'_bel that

_f_   _p_

swim or to ford! Old Stonewall, still watching, prays low to the Lord: "Good

leans on his sword, _And while we are mounting prays low to the Lord: "Now

Bye dear old Re bel! the ri vers not wide, _And Mary_land's lights in her

each cav__a___lier that loves Hon or and Right, Let him follow the feather of

28

window to guide." Come tigh...ten your girth and slacken your rein; Come

Stuart to night!" Come tigh...ten your girth and slacken your rein; Come

buc...kle your blanket and holster a_gain; Try the click of your trigger and

buc...kle your blanket and holster a_gain; Try the click of your trigger and

cres

balance your blade For he must ride sure that goes Ri...ding a Raid!

balance your blade For he must ride sure that goes Ri...ding a Raid!

Verse 3

There's a man in a white house with blood on his mouth!
If there's Knaves in the North, there are braves in the South.
We are three thousand horses, and not one afraid;
We are three thousand sabres, and not a dull blade.
Come tighten your girth and slacken your rein;
Come buckle your blanket and holster again.
Try the click of your trigger and balance your blade.
For he must ride sure that goes Riding a Raid.
Chorus. Come tighten &c.

Verse 4

Then gallop, then gallop by ravines and rocks!
Who would bar us the way take his toll in hard knocks;
For with these points of steel, on the line of Penn,
We have made some fine strokes – and we'll make 'em again.
Then tighten your girth and slacken your rein;
Come buckle your blanket and holster again;
Try the click of your trigger and balance your blade
For he must ride sure, that goes Riding a Raid.
Chorus Then tighten &c.

29

Gen. Nathan B. Forrest, C.S.A.

"Whacking sword" used by Forrest's troopers.

3

Western Riders

WHILE LEE had been occupied with the defense of the Confederate capital, his success had been more than offset by events in the west, that vast theater that lay beyond the Appalachians. A swift Confederate wooing of the border states of Missouri and Kentucky had been quickly followed by bitter warfare, with the possession of the war's principal objectives, the railroads and the great rivers, as the prize.

Here, as in the east, cavalry played an important part; here, also, talented leaders of cavalry appeared first on the Southern side. Most picturesque of these was forty-year-old Nathan Bedford Forrest who had enlisted as a private in June 1861. A product of poverty and the life of the wilderness, he was able to say afterwards: "I went into the army worth a million and a half dollars, and came out a beggar." A month after he enlisted he put the following advertisement in the *Memphis Daily Appeal:*

"A chance for active service . . . Having been authorized by Governor Harris to raise a battalion of mounted rangers . . . I desire to enlist 500 . . . mounted and equipped with such arms as they can procure (shotguns and pistols preferable)."

Beyond what his recruits were able to bring into the service with them, he outfitted his battalion as best he knew how, paying for their equipment out of his own pocket. He was deadly serious. "War," he said, "means fighting, and fighting means killing"; and the deadliest weapons he knew were firearms. Firearms were, moreover, the weapons his men knew best. Here, even more than in the eastern South, the saber was unknown and distrusted. In many Confederate cavalry units in the west sabers were not carried at all, except by the officers as a badge of rank. Even when they charged, it was with pistol or carbine in hand; and the nature of the country was such that dismounted action was by far the more frequent.

Gen. Joseph Shelby, C.S.A.
This Kentucky-born cavalry leader was active in almost every campaign of the war west of the Mississippi River.

By February, 1862, Forrest had joined forces with the troops gathering at Fort Donelson, which had been grubbed from the Cumberland's west bank just below the Kentucky line and ten miles east of its opposite number, Fort Henry, on the Tennessee River. Federal General U. S. Grant had moved his force up the Tennessee River to capture Fort Henry on February 6. Forcing Forrest back on Fort Donelson, Grant invested that fort to cut off its garrison's possible escape toward Nashville.

Guns guarded Tennessee's capitol at Nashville.

Col. John Hunt Morgan, C.S.A.

As infantry began fighting infantry on the 13th, Forrest was "everywhere along the lines during the day . . . attending closely to the duties of observation which devolved upon him," and on the 15th, in bitter cold, his battalion led General G. J. Pillow's counterattack which threw back Grant's right far enough to uncover a route for escape. But that midnight Forrest was called to headquarters. "To his amazement," he found the fort's commanders "discussing the surrender of the army." "I told them," he recorded, "that I neither could nor would surrender my command. General Pillow then said I could cut my way out."

An hour later Forrest was leading his regiment out through the backwaters to Nashville, while, on the 16th, "Unconditional Surrender" made prisoners of more than 10,000 Confederate troops. "It was a blow that staggered the Confederacy, and from which it is safe to say it never fully recovered," said John Wyeth, one of Forrest's soldiers. Nashville fell a week later.

Federal divisions were rushed through this, the first break in the defense wall of the Confederacy. Up the Tennessee they went to Pittsburg Landing and Shiloh Church, close to the Mississippi state line. There General Albert Sidney Johnston attacked them on April 6th, and was repulsed, losing his own life. Although General William Tecumseh Sherman pressed upon the retreating Confederates, Forrest had at least the satisfaction of demonstrating what his cavalry could do against a victorious enemy. "The enemy's cavalry came down boldly at a charge, led by General Forrest in person, breaking through our line of skirmishers," wrote a witness of that action; "the regiment of infantry broke . . . threw away their muskets and fled. . . . Forrest is the very devil."

Of gentler upbringing, born in Alabama and raised in bluegrass Kentucky, was John Hunt Morgan, who was destined to be Jeb Stuart's western counterpart. Like Forrest, he had recruited his own command and began the war in a buffer zone in front of the infantry in Tennessee and Kentucky. General P. G. T. Beauregard, commander at First Manassas and again at Shiloh, after A. S. Johnston's

33

Col. Walter P. Lane, 3rd Texas (South Kansas-Texas) Cavalry, c.s.a.

Gen. Frederick Steele, u.s.a.

death, had seen enough of Captain Morgan at the latter battle "to reveal a great innate talent to his practiced eye." He determined to make use of it. Morgan was promoted to colonel and sent off to harass the enemy in middle Tennessee and Kentucky.

Other Southern cavalry leaders had distinguished themselves by this time. In the campaigns of Major General Sterling Price in Arkansas and Missouri, the cavalry brigade organized by Brigadier General Joseph Orville Shelby made a brilliant record for their leader. His skill and courage, both in raiding and in the battles at Carthage, Wilson's Creek, Lexington, Springfield, and Pea Ridge, gave his

men an indestructable confidence. In March 1862, at Pea Ridge, W. P. Lane's Third Texas Cavalry grumbled as they covered the Confederate withdrawal: "The enemy were too crippled to follow us." But the result was a pattern of fighting that would afflict this area until the war's end—raid and counter raid.

During this same month of March, on the Federal side, General H. W. Halleck, commander of the Department of the Missouri, dispatched Major General Frederick Steele to raid Confederate stores at Pocahontas, Arkansas. "Destroy all enemy stores not required for your use," ran his orders; "then go to Jacksonport . . . Batesville . . . Helena . . . Success will depend in a great measure on the rapidity of your movements . . . If you find the enemy in too large force to attack at any place, you will fall back." By early 1864 Steele had an excellent force of 15,000 men. But Shelby's troopers, who by that time numbered only 1000, held them up for a whole day.

Unique among western cavalry were Federal Alfred Ellett's "horse marines." Formed to stop the Confederate guerrilla warfare along the banks of the Tennessee and Cumberland soon after Shiloh, these river-boat horsemen were under orders to go ashore at any point from which shots were fired and destroy everything of value in the vicinity, including houses "supposed to be" affording shelter to guerrillas. Seven steamboats were detailed to Ellett, each stabling horses on the main deck, with their riders and an infantry support billeted above. The boats were of light draft, usually no more than three feet, which allowed them to run in close to muddy banks where landing stages were swung out and the horses could trot ashore.

Gen. Alfred W. Ellett, U.S.A.

Along the Tennessee River, a transport fleet.

36

Gen. Edward R. S. Canby, U.S.A.

In Texas the cavalry in the expedition commanded by H. H. Sibley, which rode out from Fort Bliss in early 1862, won little renown. Poorly equipped from lack of funds and with its ranks thinned by smallpox and pneumonia, it threatened Fort Craig in New Mexico in mid-February by drawing up on the open plain in "Alexandrian" fashion and offering battle. To Sibley's surprise "the challenge was disregarded"; and when he managed to draw the enemy out shortly after, the combat, at Valverde, was indecisive.

Sibley occupied Albuquerque and nearby Fort Marcy. But he was unable to obtain adequate supplies, so that when General Edward R. S. Canby attacked with Federal reinforcements, including the hard-riding First Colorado Cavalry, Sibley was forced to evacuate his position. A part of Canby's force failed to defeat the Confederates at Glorietta Pass,

Brig. Gen. Henry H. Sibley, C.S.A.

Federal cavalry guard a supply train near Chattanooga.

Fort Marcy, Santa Fe, was headquarters for the Union's Department of
New Mexico.

which was known to the Northerners as
Apache Canyon, but captured and destroyed
the Confederates' indispensible wagon-train;
as a result, Sibley's command was compelled
to retreat down the Rio Grande in a state that
bordered on demoralization. Sibley blamed
lack of public support for his failure. "The
citizens," he said, "had no distinct sentiment

Lt. Col. Samuel F. Tappan, 1st Colorado Cavalry, U.S.A.

or opinion on the vital question at issue . . . New Mexico is not worth a quarter of the blood and treasure expended in its conquest." Canby reported to Washington: "I do not apprehend another invasion of this country"; and he was right.

Another cavalryman of the western South was more fortunate. He was to win a place among the most famous cavalry leaders of the war. He was diminutive "Fighting Joe" Wheeler, "the gamest little banty I ever seen," a rural acquaintance described him. "He warn't afraid of nuthin' or nobody." A West Pointer, Wheeler was more receptive to orders than citizen-soldiers Forrest and Morgan; and he had earned the command of a brigade of cavalry by July 1862, when he slipped into western Tennessee.

"With but 500 cavalry much worn and jaded by previous service . . . we had penetrated some 70 miles behind the enemy's lines, destroyed the railroad bridges in his rear, and met him in eight separate engagements, in all of which, except [one] . . . he was thoroughly defeated."

While the Southern newspapers were exulting in the exploits of their western raiders, the rise of new Union army commanders in that region engaged the attention of the readers of the Northern papers. The slovenly dressed U. S. Grant, the belligerent little Irish Phil Sheridan, and William Tecumseh Sherman, who had been scoffed at for predicting that the war would last more than three months, had been making the headlines.

Meanwhile, President Lincoln had relieved "Old Brains" Halleck of his command at St. Louis and appointed him to succeed Winfield Scott, veteran of the War of 1812, as General-in-Chief of the Federal armies.

39

Gen. Thomas Rosser, C.S.A.

4

Jeb Stuart Raids North

Confederate Carbine,
calibre .58, made by J. P. Murray,
Columbia, S. C.

THE POOR SHOWING of the armies under Frémont, Banks, and McDowell against Stonewall Jackson in northern Virginia had caused Lincoln to combine them in June 1862, under a commander from the west. This was John Pope, of whom it was said later that he "had all of Mr. Lincoln's garrulity . . . and none of that good old man's unassuming common sense." He had, however, captured New Madrid in Missouri and Island Number Ten on the Mississippi by a brilliant stroke; and when Jackson encountered a part of his force at Cedar Mountain on August 9, it looked as if Pope might again have his own way. But Lee's main forces began to arrive; a captured order revealed the Confederate plan for cutting his communications by a raid of Stuart's cavalry; and Pope shifted his position to the north side of the Rappahannock.

41

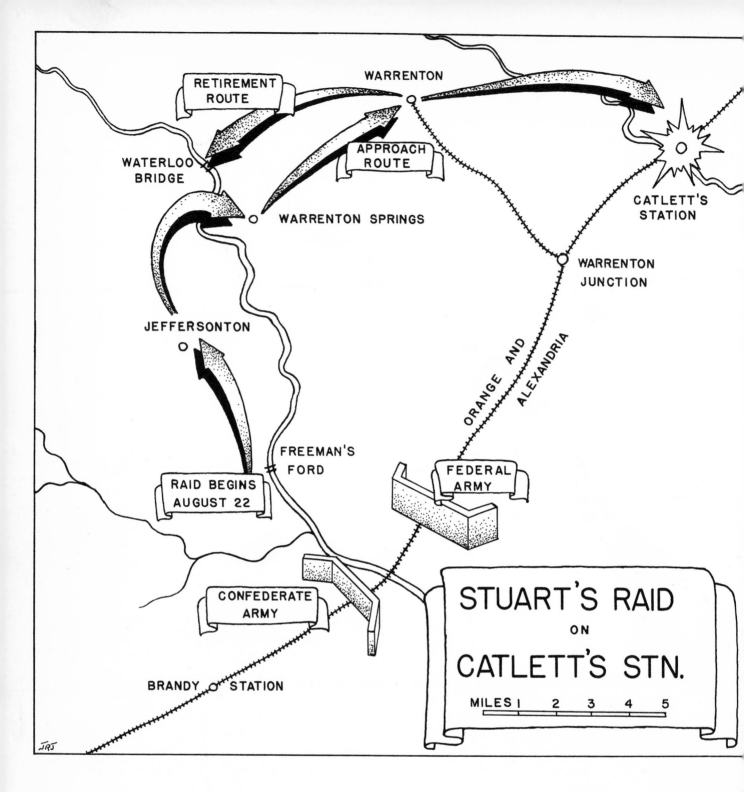

RETIREMENT ROUTE

WARRENTON

WATERLOO BRIDGE

APPROACH ROUTE

WARRENTON SPRINGS

CATLETT'S STATION

WARRENTON JUNCTION

JEFFERSONTON

ORANGE AND ALEXANDRIA

FREEMAN'S FORD

FEDERAL ARMY

RAID BEGINS AUGUST 22

CONFEDERATE ARMY

STUART'S RAID
ON
CATLETT'S STN.

MILES 1   2   3   4   5

BRANDY STATION

Stuart wished to strike Pope's rear. On August 22 Lee approved his plan. Breaking away in mid-morning from an artillery duel across the Rappahannock at Freeman's Ford, Jeb led a raiding party, with two pieces of artillery, toward Catlett's Station on the Orange and Alexandria Railroad. Crossing the river, he galloped into Warrenton in the early afternoon; and, while he halted there for his column to close up, he learned that there were no Federals nearby. So he crossed Cedar Creek and rode down its east bank "with the view to destroy the railroad bridge near Catlett's . . . the telegraph line, and thus cut the enemy's line of communication."

An evening thunderstorm struck, with rain "driven almost horizontally with such stinging force that it was impossible to keep a horse's head to the blast." The advance party commander, Tom Rosser, galloped into "the darkest night I ever saw," as Stuart told it, to capture Catlett's before penetrating the Federal camp. Luck was with the raiders: Jeb captured a Negro who had known him before the war, and the man led them "boldly to within a few feet of the tents occupied by the convivial staff of General Pope."

A bugle touched off "a roar like Niagara" as 2000 Rebels "came thundering on," the horsemen firing wildly into the elegantly furnished tents, lighted by handsome lamps." One Federal officer had just lifted a glass of toddy, remarking, "now this is something like

Gen. Thomas "Stonewall" Jackson, C.S.A.

comfort. I hope Jeb Stuart won't disturb us tonight." Next instant he had dropped it, shouting, "There he is, by God!"

One soaked rider remembered stopping to laugh as the tents erupted with men, some of

Catlett's Station on the Orange and Alexandria Railroad. Here Stuart's yelling and shooting troopers rode through the tents of Pope's staff one gay night.

Union guns guard Chain Bridge to Washington against Virginia raiders.

the tents trapping their occupants "in their fall like fish in a net, within whose folds we could trace the struggling outlines of frantic men." One detachment struck the depot, cutting down riflemen with their sabers, "leaping their horses upon the low platform and crashing right into the front room."

Meanwhile, Colonels Rosser and L. T. Brian flushed most of McDowell's staff to scattered wagons, where they rallied to hold off their attackers. Stuart had not forgotten his main object here, the destruction of the Cedar Creek trestle. But when W. C. Wickham's Fourth Virginia approached it, they found it thick with Federal infantry waiting for targets. Stuart decided against furnishing any. Since he had with him most of the cavalry, which was vital to the army, he decided not to risk staying any longer. The storm had turned Cedar Creek and the Rappahannock into torrents. So, gathering his detachments, he rode back the way he had come.

Stuart was frustrated by not accomplishing the job he had set for himself, but his spirits

soared at dawn when he surveyed his captures of more than 300 prisoners, including Pope's field quartermaster, the general's uniforms and personal baggage, and money chests containing $520,000; "but what was of peculiar value was the dispatch book of General Pope, which contained information of great importance to us, throwing light upon the strength, movements, and designs of the enemy."

"Subsequent events," Stuart was pleased to report later, "have shown what a demoralizing effect the success of this expedition had upon the army of the enemy, shaking their confidence in a general who scorned the enterprise and ridiculed the courage of his adversaries . . . and it compelled him to look to his communications and make heavy detachments from his main body to protect them. . . . Our own loss was slight." Four were killed and one wounded.

More immediately important were Pope's captured papers revealing that his 45,000 troops would be reinforced by 20,000 within two days, and within five days more by the Army of the Potomac from the Peninsula, bringing the Federal strength to nearly 130,000. Lee, with his 55,000, would have to move quickly to counteract this numerical superiority.

Lee's plan was to strike at Pope's rear with half his army under Jackson while Stuart made a wide turning movement to the left. Pope had unconsciously invited such a stroke when, on assuming command of his new army, he had chastised his subordinates with orders that they must face and stand up to the enemy instead of worrying about "lines of retreat" and "bases of supply."

"I left Jeffersonton on the morning of the 25th to throw my command between Washington City and the army of General Pope," wrote Jackson. ". . . At Gainesville I was joined by General Stuart . . . He kept upon my right flank during the residue of the day.

44

My command was now in the rear of General Pope's army."

Pope had seen Jackson's force shifting northwest and later claimed, "The movement of Jackson . . . while the main body of the enemy confronted me . . . was well known to me. . . . I knew that this movement was no raid." Hindsight had helped him write this report, for he had taken little action to protect his flank and rear. Instead: "I confidently relied upon the forces which I had been assured would be sent from Alexandria."

The movement's first effect upon him was at Bristoe Station, between Catlett's and Manassas, when Colonel Thomas T. Mumford's Second Virginia Cavalry tried to trap the two garrison companies. The enemy cavalry "scampered away with their horses. Many of the infantry fled to the hotel . . . and opened fire." Since "it was about the time the evening trains from Pope's army had been in the habit of passing," it was decided to take advantage of this situation. Switches were thrown, and as a train rushed past, volleys were fired into its sides. The surprised engineer put on more steam. "Down the embankment rushed the engine, screaming and hissing, and down upon it rushed the cars, piling up one upon another until the pile reached higher than the embankment, checking further additions to its con-

Railroad men, righting an engine thrown over the bank when raiders wrecked the track, pause for the photographer.

45

Supply wagons cross Middle Bridge over Antietam Creek, scene of bitter fighting during the battle of Sharpsburg.

fused heap, and arresting the rear half of the train upon the track." Minutes later another train piled into the wreck.

Jackson's "habit in the Valley had been to make enforced requisitions upon the Federal commissaries for his subsistance supplies; and the tempting opportunity of continuing this policy and rationing his hungry command" caused Brigadier General Trimble to propose that he lead his Twenty-first Carolina and Georgia infantry regiments against the Federal supply bases at Manassas. They had already marched thirty miles since dawn, but every man, said Trimble, "set out with cheerful alacrity to perform the service." A few minutes later, "in order to increase the prospect of success," Jackson ordered Stuart to assume command of the mission. Unfortunately, however, General Trimble was not informed of this.

Sending some squadrons to the rear of Manassas to block the garrison's escape, Stuart pushed forward rapidly. But the enemy had been alerted. The Federals allowed him to advance "until challenged by [their] interior sentinels" and then received him with "a fire of cannister." "As the infantry were near, coming on," he explained later, "I awaited its arrival as it was too dark to venture cavalry over uncertain ground against artillery. I directed General Trimble . . . to rest his center directly on the railroad and advance upon the place. . . . He soon sent word it was so dark he preferred waiting until morning, which I accordingly directed he should do. As soon as day broke the place was taken without much difficulty."

But the few shots exchanged here were insignificant compared with Trimble's verbal blast when he learned that Stuart's report understated the work of the infantry. "As to the statement . . . that the place was taken without much difficulty," bridled Trimble, "I am embarrassed by a difficulty in applying the compliment to myself or him, but will . . . admit it was taken without difficulty so far as his exertions contributed to its capture."

Stuart retaliated with: "There seems to be a growing tendency to abuse and underrate the services of that arm of service [cavalry] by a few officers of infantry, among whom I regret to find General Trimble." The exchange was as unnecessary as it was regrettable, for there was glory enough for all. The captures included 300 prisoners, 200 railroad cars, a like number of horses, eight cannon, four sutler's stores, and "many millions of quartermaster and commissary stores."

To Jackson's men, who arrived during the morning after living on roasted corn during their fifty-six-mile hike of the past two days, the twenty-five tons of captured bacon was fantastic. Even Trimble's guards, posted according to Jackson's policy, could not stop them. One of A. P. Hill's men wrote to his wife: "To see a starving man eating lobster salad and drinking Rhine wine, barefooted

The note on the above pencil sketch reads: "Rebel Cavalry under Stuart burning the bridge over the Catocktin creek under pretense of checking the pursuit, but in reality to destroy the fine new barn and property of Adam Coogle a Union Maryland farmer. Our cavalry immediately forded the stream and continued the pursuit."

Gen. Matthew C. Butler, C.S.A.

and in tatters, was curious; the whole thing incredible."

Under the impression that the Confederates were hit-and-run raiders, the First New Jersey rode in from Alexandria and demanded a surrender. They were answered with a blast from the captured Union guns; their brigadier was killed; and as a Confederate soldier told it, "We hunted that New Jersey brigade like scattered partridges."

Of the events of the next few days General Pope's cautious recollection ran: "As soon as it became known to me that Jackson was on the railroad it became apparent that the upper Rappahannock was no longer tenable. . . . I accordingly evacuated at once." The move precipitated the Second Battle of Manassas, when "all day long," wrote a Southerner, "they

Stuart's horsemen leave Chambersburg, Pa., October 11, 1862, having accepted the surrender of the town.

48

Stuart, with 1800 troopers, crossed the Potomac at McCoy's Ford, raiding the North.

threw their masses at us; all day they fell back shattered and shrieking." By September 3 Pope had his army behind the outer defenses of Washington. Two days later he was relieved. "He appeared not again."

Lee realized that the Confederate policy of a defensive war must be given up, and that here was an opportunity to do so. If he stood his ground, all he could do was stop another invasion. But at Washington now they were throwing up additional entrenchments, and the War Department was calling in much of its army to defend the capital. To be sure, as he notified President Davis, he lacked adequate material and the means of transportation, and his men were ragged and, many of them, shoeless; but their spirit made up for these deficiencies.

If he could tear up the Baltimore and Ohio Railroad through Maryland and the Pennsyl-vania Railroad through Pennsylvania, most of the Union communications with the west would be cut. The movement would transfer the war from improverished Virginia; and enemy territory would furnish the mountain of supplies of which his army stood in dire need.

With Stuart's untiring horsemen covering their movement, the Confederate army began crossing the Potomac on September 4. Jackson captured Harper's Ferry, and Stuart's cavalry did their best to delay the march of the Federal army—once more under McClellan's command—as it toiled up the Potomac's northern bank to head off Lee's thrust at Pennsylvania. It was just in time. At Sharpsburg on Antietam Creek on September 17, McClellan inflicted on the Confederate army a loss of 8000 men, and Lee fell back across the river.

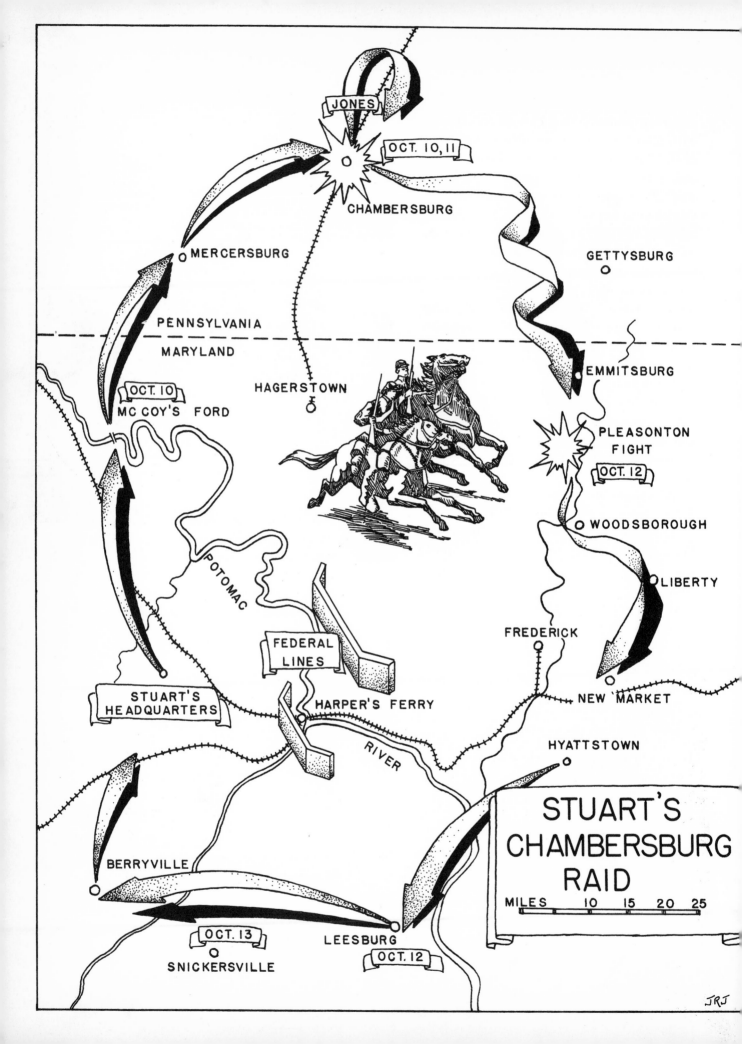

JONES

OCT. 10, 11

CHAMBERSBURG

GETTYSBURG

MERCERSBURG

PENNSYLVANIA

MARYLAND

EMMITSBURG

OCT. 10

HAGERSTOWN

PLEASONTON
FIGHT

MC COY'S FORD

OCT. 12

WOODSBOROUGH

LIBERTY

POTOMAC

FREDERICK

FEDERAL
LINES

STUART'S
HEADQUARTERS

HARPER'S FERRY

NEW MARKET

RIVER

HYATTSTOWN

STUART'S
CHAMBERSBURG
RAID

MILES   10   15   20   25

BERRYVILLE

OCT. 13

LEESBURG

OCT. 12

SNICKERSVILLE

JRJ

McClellan, however, hesitated to follow him; and when General Alfred Pleasonton's cavalry, with infantry support, assailed Stuart south of the Potomac on October 1, the movement was a failure. "The enemy retreated in a panic," according to W. W. Blackford of the Confederate forces, "followed at full speed by our cavalry, and we drove them across the river at Shepherdstown in great confusion."

Now the Southern infantry rested, but the Southern cavalry roved, for McClellan must be kept on edge. "You will," read Lee's orders to Stuart, "form a detachment of well-mounted men . . . cross the Potomac above Williamsport . . . proceed to the rear of Chambersburg and endeavor to destroy the railroad bridge over the branch of the Conococheague. Any other damage . . . you will also execute . . . gain all information of the position, force, and probable intention of the enemy which you can."

At daylight on October 10, Stuart led 1800 of his horsemen across McCoy's Ford against "some little opposition." After capturing a Federal signal station on top of a mountain on the Hagerstown-Hancock turnpike, he reached Mercersburg by midnight. "I was extremely anxious to reach Hagerstown, where large supplies were stored, but was satisfied . . . that the notice that the enemy had of my approach . . . would enable him to prevent my capturing it. I therefore turned toward Chambersburg." They had indeed been notified, and McClellan's cavalry chief Pleasonton issued orders to trap the insolent Confederate raider. He led in person a detachment of 400 men from Knoxville, Maryland, for that purpose.

When Stuart's vanguard arrived at Chambersburg it was dark and raining, but he "did not deem it safe to defer the attack until morning." He sent a detachment of Colonel M. C. Butler's Second Carolina into the town, and three citizens came forward to accept the demand for unconditional surrender. "Our

The market at Carlisle, Pa., 1862. The citizens were astonished to find themselves within reach of Confederate cavalry.

people," wrote the editor of the local newspaper, "were confounded with astonishment at the brilliant audacity of the rebels penetrating twenty miles in General McClellan's rear. . . . General Hampton . . . assured us that he would scrupulously protect citizens. . . . He would take such private property as he needed for his government or troops, but would allow no wanton destruction."

Meanwhile Stuart put his men to work to do the job they had come for. "About 275 sick and wounded in hospital were paroled. During the day a large number of horses of citizens were seized and brought along. The wires were cut, and the railroad obstructed." Colonel

At Emmitsburg, Stuart's column was welcomed "with enthusiastic demonstrations of joy" by the sympathetic Marylanders.

The Farmer's Inn and Hotel in Emmitsburg was a welcome sight to Stuart's weary troopers after nearly three days in the saddle.

"Grumble" Jones was sent up the railroad toward Carlisle to destroy a trestle work; but accomplished little, for it was built of iron.

One rebel squad spent the night "on the turnpike in front of my door," a citizen related. "In a little while, one entered the yard, came up to me, and, after a profound bow, politely asked for a few coals to start a fire. I supplied him and informed him . . . where he would find wood conveniently, as I had dim visions of camp fires made of my palings. I was thanked in return, and the mild-mannered villain proceeded at once to strip the fence and kindle fires."

Stuart was interested in larger fires. He spent the Saturday morning burning 5000 muskets, a stockpile of army clothing, the machine shops, the depot, and several loaded trains. Then, swinging east toward Gettysburg to mislead pursuit, he headed south to Emmitsburg, "where, as we passed, we were hailed by the inhabitants with most enthusiastic demonstrations of joy."

52

The hardest part of the raid was still before the raiders. "From a point about forty miles in rear of the enemy we were to march to a crossing of the Potomac ten or fifteen miles below his position, passing within ten miles of his main body. . . . The march was the longest without a halt I have ever experienced . . . ninety miles with only one halt of half an hour to feed the horses the evening of the first day." And to the fatigue was added grinding anxiety. "It seemed incredible," said Blackford, "that the enemy should not have discovered our position as the day wore on. Why their cavalry had not hung upon our rear and given intelligence of our route is unaccountable."

Sgt. Daniel R. Cole, Co. D, 3rd Indiana Cavalry, U.S.A.

Pleasonton encountered Stuart's advance party west of the Monocacy on Sunday morning. "Some skirmishing took place," the Federal commander recorded, but "the enemy opened with a couple of guns, which forced my men to retire. . . . My command was not well closed up and many were unable to join their companies before the enemy had crossed the river."

Stuart had finished his second ride around McClellan. On November 5 President Lincoln wrote: "It is ordered that Major General McClellan be relieved."

Shepherdstown, W. Va., and its destroyed bridge.

Gen. John Hunt Morgan, C.S.A., and Mrs. Morgan.

5

Christmas Behind the Federal Lines

THE SECOND DECEMBER of the war was a busy month for both armies. But the Federal cavalry were so inactive that the gray riders seemed to have a monopoly of mounted operations. In the western theater Joe Wheeler now commanded all Braxton Bragg's Confederate cavalry. Although J. H. Morgan and N. B. Forrest were both ten years older than the twenty-six-year-old Wheeler, they were his loyal subordinates, content to co-operate with him because of the active employment that he gave them.

Morgan, rested after Bragg's abortive invasion of Kentucky in the previous summer and his own raids, descended on the Federal garrison at Hartsville, on December 7. Arming some of his weaponless men with captured rifles, he fought his way south again across the Cumberland, through the blocking force of Colonel (future Supreme Court Justice) John Harlan to Murfreesboro, and received a brigadier general's commission for his exploit.

Forrest, guarding Bragg's right flank, swept out of Columbia, Tennessee, on December 11, and into Lexington. "We routed them completely," ran the report, "capturing the two guns and 148 prisoners including Col. [R. G.] Ingersoll . . . about 70 horses. . . . At Webb's

Flag "From the Ladies of Charlottesville to Stuart's Horse Artillery, Our Brave Defenders."

55

Sergeant D. M. Hurt, Company K, 106th Illinois Infantry. K Company was involved in the skirmish with Forrest at the Forked Deer River railroad crossing.

Col. John M. Harlan, U.S.A.
(later Supreme Court Justice).

Station [captured] 101 Federals. . . . Advanced on Jackson . . . Trenton and Humbolt . . . prisoners over 1200."

Grant was put out. "This cut me off from all communications with the north," he complained. Worse still, Confederate cavalryman General Earl Van Dorn descended on Grant's supply base at Holly Springs, Mississippi, on December 20, "burned up all the quartermaster's stores . . . [to the value of] $1,500,000 . . . [and captured] about 1,500 prisoners." Grant was furious: "All our munitions of war, food, and forage. The capture was a disgraceful one."

He had been heading for Vicksburg with a good chance of taking it.

On December 20, Morgan left his bride of six days at her home in Murfreesboro and was away on the first of his "Christmas raids." By Christmas Day he was through Glasgow, Kentucky. On the 27th, Elizabethtown's 600-man garrison surrendered to him, and the same day his men began burning the Louisville and Nashville Railroad trestles at Muldraugh's Hill south of Louisville. Eluding all pursurers, his weary command again approached the Kentucky-Tennessee line, as Bragg fought a losing battle against Union General William Starke Rosecrans at Stones River in the outskirts of Murfreesboro. In consequence Bragg had to retreat to Tullahoma. Defeat taught him the error of fighting with one arm tied behind him—nearly half of his cavalry off raiding.

Jeb Stuart had lost that famous plumed hat of his in the Second Manassas campaign, but he was still hitting his stride in Virginia the winter of 1862–63. Fighting down his personal sorrow at the death of his little daughter, he had been blocking superior enemy forces in the gaps of the Shenandoah. He was on hand to direct his young horse artilleryman, "the Gallant Pelham," against the advance of the Federal left the morning of December 13, at Fredericksburg, when the attempt of McClellan's successor General Ambrose Burnside to storm the heights across the Rappahannock was halted with losses that shocked the North.

Now Stuart's horsemen were hovering around the enemy on watch for the next Federal move. "Stuart's men—and therefore Johnny—" wrote a Richmond mother on Christmas Eve, "have been out in all this freezing weather for fifty-six hours at a time, without food or sleep. Poor Johnny! If they

Shattered caisson at Fredericksburg, Va.

When Stuart cantered into Warrenton his troubadour, "Sweeney," led the singing column.

will only give him a furlough at Christmas, won't we feast him!"

There were no furloughs for Stuart's men that Christmas. They had entered the war singing: "If you want to have a good time, jine the cavalry." But they had changed it by this time to: "If you want to smell hell, jine the cavalry." Johnny was already riding north again. On Christmas Day Stuart was leading him and his comrades across Kelly's Ford. Two days later he had them spread out so as to cut off fifteen miles of the main road to Washington behind the Federal lines. By nightfall on the 28th he was at Burke's Station, less than fifteen miles from the Federal capital. His

raiders took over all military facilities so silently and efficiently that the telegraph operator, who was busy transcribing messages from General Heintzelman's headquarters at Alexandria, had no time to send off an alarm.

Substituting a telegraph operator of his own, Stuart wired to U. S. Quartermaster-General Meigs a complaint about the poor quality of the Federal mules he had captured: they were so slow in moving the captured wagons. Swinging westward to Warrenton, he was home again by New Year's Eve, his personal "jongleur" Sweeny leading the singing at the head of the column as it marched in. Those full choruses were characteristic of all he did.

He was wont to charge with a song on his lips, like Taillefer at Hastings. He flaunted a pair of golden spurs that some Baltimore ladies had given him and sometimes wrote K. G. S. after his name—for Knight of the Golden Spurs—when signing letters to friends.

Now he left Major E. V. White's Thirty-fifth Virginia Cavalry Battalion behind him, "on detached service . . . in the rear of the enemy," to dampen Federal holiday spirits in northern Virginia and southern Maryland with a raid of its own. White captured some pickets in Loudoun County and, "learning that there was a force of about 60 cavalry in Poolesville [Maryland] . . . sent a squad of men to watch the enemy at Harper's Ferry. They charged the pickets, capturing 26. . . . Arrived at Poolesville about 8 p.m. . . . Divided my force and charged it in two directions. . . . We captured 21."

Gen. Samuel P. Heintzelman, U.S.A.

Catlett's Station, Virginia, 1862.

59

Col. Elijah V. White, 35th Battalion, Virginia Cavalry, C.S.A.

One of Stuart's aides and scouts was a brash young lawyer from Bristol, Virginia, named John Singleton Mosby, whom one admiring Federal called "the only perfect success in the Southern army." During this Christmas raid Mosby obtained permission to remain in northern Virginia and organize a partisan band under the provisions of the April 1861 Partisan Ranger Law, which, according to its author, was an "application of the prize principle of nautical warfare to land war." The prospect of loot was "a powerful magnet to adventuresome spirits"; and there would be no complaints from the regular army when Federal quartermasters supplied Mosby's band. "I cannot recall an instance when we rejected what was on hand," said one partisan, ". . . or when we threatened to take our trade to some competitor."

Beginning operations with only nine men, Mosby soon found that his band attracted scores. Probably no other command had such varied backgrounds as his "conglomerates." Farmers and regulars on leave would join for one or two raids, while the permanent nucleus of regularly enrolled partisans, Federal deserters, and foreign volunteers carried on a steady warfare. The Forty-third Virginia Cavalry Battalion, as it came to be designated, eventually mustered close to 1000, but a raid with more than 300 men was unusual. They soon discarded sabers and rifles as impractical for their missions and fought with the .44 Colt revolver. "Some few, who could afford it . . . wore an extra pair in their saddle holsters or stuck into their boot legs. . . . Frequent practice had made every man a good shot."

Refusing combat when faced with an unfavorable situation, the foxy lawyer would fade his band into the Virginia mountains. The farmers willingly provided quarters for them. "The men select their own boarding house, restricted only to certain limits. The idea of

Col. John Singleton Mosby, 43rd Battalion, Virginia Cavalry, C.S.A.

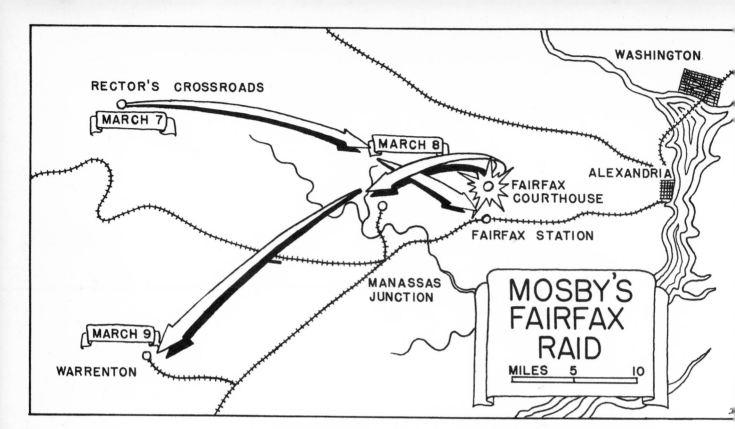

RECTOR'S CROSSROADS

MARCH 7

WASHINGTON.

MARCH 8

FAIRFAX COURTHOUSE

ALEXANDRIA

FAIRFAX STATION

MANASSAS JUNCTION

MOSBY'S FAIRFAX RAID

MILES 5 10

MARCH 9

WARRENTON

62

Five of Mosby's riders.

Mosby reported to Stuart: "At Fairfax Court House a few nights ago I captured 29 sutler's wagons, about 100 prisoners and 140 horses. I had brought all off safely near Aldie, where I fell in with a large force of the enemy's cavalry, who recaptured them."

The courthouse at Fairfax, Va. Here Mosby made life miserable for the
1st New Jersey Cavalry.

making coffee, frying bacon, or soaking hard-tack was never entertained," said ranger John Munson. "When we wanted to eat we stopped at a friendly farm house." So complete was the co-operation of the local inhabitants, indeed, that Fairfax, Fauquier, and Loudoun counties won the name of "Mosby's Confederacy."

Shortly after beginning operations as a partisan leader Mosby captured the pickets of Colonel Percy Wyndham's First New Jersey Cavalry on the Washington outpost line at Fairfax Court House. Wyndham, a Britisher, "a stalwart man, with huge mustaches, cavalry boots adorned with spurs worthy of a caballero, slouched hat and plume," had been captured once and exchanged [as Mosby had

been]. He now tried hard to brighten a rather dull record. In pursuit "with some 200 men . . . some 27 miles beyond my pickets, at Middleburg," said Wyndham, "I came up with them, and after a short skirmish, captured 24."

He neglected to identify twenty-one of his prisoners as civilians but, as Mosby pointed out: "The extent of the annoyance I have been to the Yankees may be judged by the fact that . . . they retaliate on citizens for my acts."

Mosby decided to conduct a retaliation of his own. "Having accurately ascertained the number and disposition of the troops in Fairfax County, I determined to make the attempt to reach Fairfax Court House, where the headquarters of that portion of the army was established." Gathering thirty-nine partisans at Rector's Crossroads on March 7, 1863, he headed for his target, making a final approach the next night during a heavy rain. "So intense was the darkness that, as we were passing through a dense body of pines, the command was separated into two divisions." But the rear portion of the column wound eastward to find Mosby waiting at a woodman's hut.

"We were now near the enemy's outside picket line between Centerville and Chantilly, and by use of great caution we succeeded in passing through without being discovered."

Col. Percy Wyndham, 1st New Jersey Cavalry, U.S.A.

Recapture of a wagon train from Mosby's men on the Little River Turnpike at Mount Zion church.

Gen. Edwin H. Stoughton, U.S.A.

Cutting telegraph lines to the southwest, the partisans rode within a mile of their target before swinging cross-country onto the Fairfax Station road to become a "Federal" patrol. In the deserted streets of Fairfax Court House a detachment under Sergeant Ames, ex-Fifth New York Cavalry, hurried "to capture Wyndham, another party . . . to collect the horses in the stables, while with a third Mosby proceeded to pay his respect to Brigadier General Stoughton," whose cavalry brigade camped in less imposing quarters six miles away.

Arousing the general's house with the shout, "Dispatches for General Stoughton," Mosby related, "I walked into his room with two of my men and shaking him in bed, said, 'General, get up.' He rose up; and, rubbing his eyes,

asked what was the meaning of all this. I replied, 'It means, sir, that Stuart's cavalry are in possession of this place, and you are a prisoner.'"

Upon herding Stoughton and his aides into the street, Mosby learned that Wyndham "had gone to Washington" to learn why General Heintzelman had blocked his resignation papers.

"After we started our return," said one trooper, "encumbered with 32 prisoners . . . and 58 horses, which were all we could bring along with us, a window of a house we passed was thrown open, and a voice imperatively demanded what command that cavalry belonged to." The challenger was Lieutenant Colonel Robert Johnstone, Fifth New York Cavalry. But when he saw the raiders running toward his door he "made his escape from them in a nude state," the lieutenant serving as post provost-marshal was pleased to report. The rangers were home before they figured out his hiding place—under the backyard privy.

Slipping southward into the pre-dawn darkness to mislead pursuit, Mosby soon turned west and passed so close to the fortifications of Centerville that he was "hailed by the sentinel on the redout, and [could] distinctly see the bristling cannon through the embrasures." Here Wyndham's adjutant, who had picked the wrong night to borrow his commander's empty bed, thought he saw a chance to escape, but a pistol shot that grazed his head made him change his mind.

Mosby swam his forces across Cub Run, which was "much swollen by the recent snows," and was reprimanded by a shivering Stoughton—anxious to be in the custody of fellow West Pointer Fitz Lee—for "the first bad treatment I have received at your hands." Crossing Bull Run at Sudley Springs Ford, over which at First Manassas the Federals had mounted their attack, Mosby struck the turnpike into Warrenton. There "acclaiming" citizens, alerted by his scouts, "prepared for our hungry band a plentiful breakfast." Shortly after, an elated Stuart praised his former scout in general orders: "His brilliant exploit [is] unparalleled in the war."

The superiority of the Confederate cavalry, both in initiative and performance, had become a sore point in the North by this time. When Lincoln replaced Burnside with "Fighting Joe" Hooker at the head of the Army of the Potomac in January 1863, he wrote to Hooker in a personal note: "I believe you to be a brave and skillful soldier. . . . Give us victories." Hooker ranted to his chief of cavalry: "You have got to stop those disgraceful cavalry surprises . . . and, by God, sir, if you don't do it . . . I will relieve the whole of you and take command of the cavalry myself!"

President Lincoln visited the headquarters of the Army of the Potomac that spring and, at Falmouth on April 9, reviewed its cavalry, with General Napoleon Bonaparte Buford riding at the head. By that time the Federal cavalry had earned the honor of his special attention. On March 17, General W. W. Averell led a force of 3000 with six guns across the Rappahannock at Kelly's Ford, "to rout or destroy" the Confederate force under Fitz Lee near Culpeper. The action was prolonged and complicated. The Confederates advanced shouting, "Draw your pistols and fight like gentlemen!" But war was war to the Yankees. When the mud of a plowed field took the impetus out of one Southern charge, the Northerners blasted it with carbine fire from a halt, without even taking the trouble to dismount. Tactically the action was a Union victory: the Confederates were greatly outnumbered. But Averell lacked the flair of the born cavalry leader. Faulty intelligence told him that he would confront enemy entrenchments and reinforcements—neither of which actually existed—if he pushed on, and he fell back across the river. The Con-

federate loss was 133, among whom was Stuart's young chief of artillery John Pelham, veteran of nearly sixty fights. "His loss is irreparable," Stuart said, and he wrote to his wife: "I want Jemmie [Jeb, Jr.] to be just like him." "With Pelham," one Southerner remembered, "there passed from the army something youthful and golden."

Behind Hooker's lines, in Mosby's Confederacy, the hit-and-run partisans continued to bother the Union army's rear. "There is now a splendid opportunity to strike the enemy in the rear of Warrenton Junction," ran a memo from Stuart to Mosby; "the trains are running regularly to that point. Capture a train and interrupt the operation of the railroad. . . . Information of the movements of large bodies is of the greatest importance to us just now."

Mosby went to work, burning all the trestles and culverts that he could find unguarded, including the Cedar Run Bridge. Assembling forty-eight "conglomerates," he allowed a squad one hour in which to learn the proper use of a borrowed howitzer, and rode for Catlett's Station. Next morning he cut the telegraph wires there, slipped out a rail, and

Gen. Napoleon Bonaparte Buford leads his division past President Lincoln during the cavalry review at Falmouth, Va., April 9, 1863.

Maj. John Pelham, C.S.A., "The Great Cannoneer."
(*mortally wounded at Kelly's Ford, March 17, 1863*)

Corbett, earned their respect when, according to his own account, he "faced and fought against a whole column of them, all alone, none but God being with me to help me, my being in a large field and they being in the road with a high board fence between us, enabled me to hold out against them as long as I did . . . They finally had the fence torn down and closed around me, and when my pistol gave out . . . I was captured." He was later exchanged and remained in the service till the end of the war. It was he who, in defiance of orders, shot and killed John Wilkes Booth, Lincoln's assassin.

Of course, all this raiding could do no more than delay the On-to-Richmond movement for

pointed the howitzer down the track. "The train came dashing along at headlong speed, and at the appointed place ran off the track. The guard, consisting of 200 infantry, opened fire upon us, but were quickly dispersed by a round of grape."

In a nearby camp an alarmed Colonel W. D. Mann "heard firing . . . and went in search with the First Vermont, Fifth New York, and a detachment of Seventh Michigan. Came up with Mosby in a strong position . . . and charged"—"in gallant style," said a waiting partisan, "and in column of fours . . . At a distance of 80 yards we opened." Mann reported four killed and eight wounded. Mosby's only death was Captain B. S. Hoskins, who had resigned a commission in the British army to join the rangers. But he lost his howitzer and at least two men taken prisoner.

Daring was not a monopoly of Mosby's men. A Sixteenth New York cavalryman, Boston

68

Sgt. "Boston" Corbett, Co. L, 16th New York Cavalry, U.S.A.

Col. William D. Mann, 7th Michigan Cavalry, U.S.A.

Sgt. Maj. Otho S. Lee, Stuart's Horse Artillery, C.S.A.

The Rappahannock Railway loses a bridge, October 13, 1863.

69

Troopers of the 13th New York Cavalry, which tangled with Mosby's rangers more than once.

A detachment of the 13th New York Cavalry was peacefully watering a drove of horses intended for the Federal army when surprised by Mosby and 35 of his men at Billy Gooding's Tavern, on the Little River Turnpike 10 miles from Alexandria. The horses were successfully stampeded in the fracas.

Gen. Joseph Hooker, U.S.A.

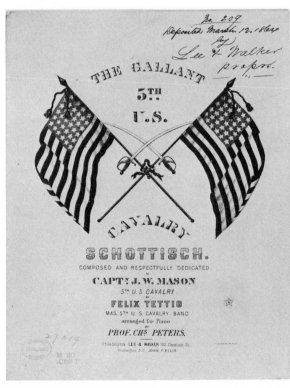

A schottisch is dedicated to the 5th U.S. Cavalry.

which Hooker was preparing his army. He had proved to be a good administrator, dealing ably with the troops' grumbles about food, furloughs, discipline, and training; and when he showed Lincoln his plan for beating Lee, the President approved it. Three moves were to be made simultaneously. George Stoneman, who had commanded the Third Corps at Fredericksburg, would take most of the available cavalry, less one division, on a raid around Lee's left, "cutting the enemy's communications with Richmond" and "checking his retreat over those lines." At the same time a feinting force would cross the Rappahannock at Fredericksburg and cause enough confusion to hold Lee in place while Hooker moved his main army upstream to Chancellorsville and into Lee's rear. "Here on this open ground [opposite Bank's Ford] I intend to fight my battle," said Hooker.

71

Gen. George Stoneman, U.S.A.

6

George Stoneman Raids South

GEORGE STONEMAN, a "lithe, severe, gristly, sanguine person, whose eyes flashed even in repose," was one of those old regulars around whom armies are built. Pegged at the halfway mark in his '46 West Point class (McClellan second and George Pickett last), Stoneman galloped straight into the Mexican War and spent the next nine years in the west, scouting and Indian fighting. He returned to his native New York when the Civil War began and spent the summer of 1861 on McClellan's staff in West Virginia.

By that August "the cavalry had been organized into a division under . . . Stoneman, Chief of Cavalry, and distributed by assignment to the corps of the army, excepting the cavalry reserve under General P. St. George Cooke and that portion which was attached to general headquarters." It was a poor system, this spreading thin of the cavalry potential. Hooker's plan was devised to correct the error. By it the horsemen would fight as a concentrated mass. It would give a chance to show Stuart's riders the caliber of the blue-coated cavalry. They had demonstrated at Kelly's Ford that in the past two years they had learned how to stay on their horses 'cross-country and fight in the saddle. Stoneman was eager to show what they could do under a first-class leader.

Taking his column upstream in the Spring of 1863, two weeks before Hooker moved his main army, Stoneman leaked word that he was after guerrillas in the Shenandoah. But heavy rains so raised the river that his crossing had to be postponed from the 13th of April to the 29th, the same day that the main army began to cross downstream. With rations and ammunition transferred to serviceable mounts, Stoneman rid his command of pack mules, wagons, and unfit men. These were sent down to Germanna "to follow in the rear of the army

Ruins of the bridge at Germanna Ford, Va.

and remain with it until we formed a junction therewith, which we expected would be in the vicinity of Richmond . . . each officer and man to take with him no more than he could carry on his horse, myself and staff setting the example."

Satisfied that his intentions were unknown to the enemy, Stoneman got his force across by late afternoon. "I assembled the . . . commanders, spread our maps, and had a thorough understanding of what we were to do,

and where we were to go." In the belief that Stuart would be occupied elsewhere, he felt more could be accomplished by breaking his force into two principal segments. "Averell [General William Woods] . . . was to push on in the direction of Culpepper Court House, and myself, with Gregg's division, Buford's reserve brigade . . . was to push toward Stevensburg. It was expected that Averell would be able to reach Brandy Station that night, driving whatever enemy there was before him, and I was to communicate with him at that point."

During the 29th, Averell engaged in "some artillery practice" with Colonel J. R. Chambliss, who had been stationed by "Rooney" Lee at Kelly's Ford. The next day some of his men found a dispatch to Chambliss that directed him to "find out what kind of troops marched down behind the wagons" across the river, for "the general is very anxious to know where to look for Stoneman, as we have heard nothing from him."

But Jeb Stuart had heard. From Brandy Station he galloped toward Germanna on the 29th, "pierced the Federal line of march, and took enough prisoners to identify the three corps, and to ascertain that the main army was behind them." Then he coolly "turned his back on Stoneman . . . and rode with Fitz Lee across the front and flank of the marching blue masses. From that day," wrote John Thomason, "Hooker was blinded." In a flurry of orders and counter-orders the Union general brought back the stalled Averell on May 3. Stoneman saw no more of Averell during his raid.

"In a cold, drenching rain," before dawn on April 30, "we started on our way," wrote Stoneman, "in a command numbering about 3500 . . . as determined a set of men as ever started on any expedition." Pushing his advance across the Rapidan below Raccoon Ford,

Troopers of Co. D, 3rd Pennsylvania Cavalry, at Brandy Station.

75

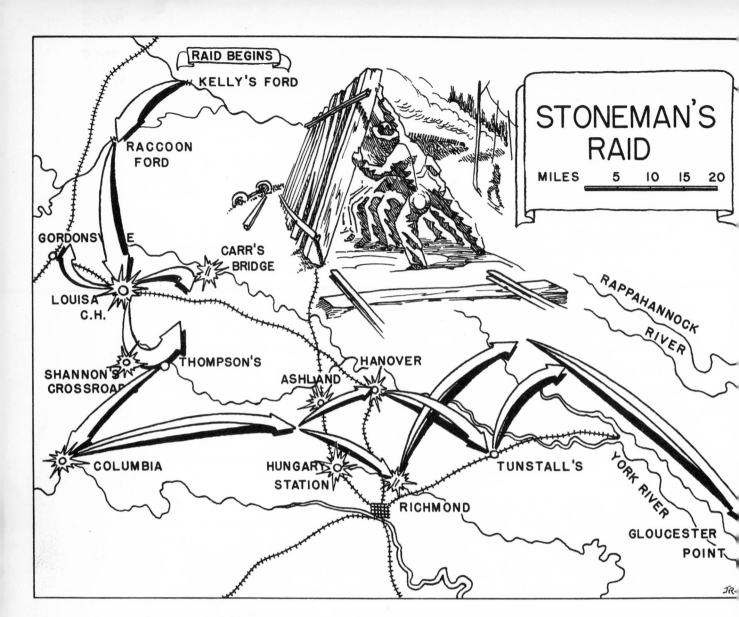

he turned to scatter the Confederate guard there and had brought his main body across the river by ten that night. After a bivouac of only four hours his troopers were again in the saddle, but a thick fog kept them waiting until daylight. "From here I pushed Gregg's division on to Louisa Court House, on the Virginia Central Railroad, where it arrived about 2 A.M., May 2."

General David M. Gregg struck the place with three columns, a flanking force on either side. But no enemy was found, and "the pio- neer corps was at once set to work destroying the railroad." The main column followed close behind to assist in wrecking all rail facilities and commissary stores. Stoneman hurried a squadron of the First Maine from Louisa to Gordonsville—where it was turned back by the Ninth Virginia—and dispatched the First U. S. Cavalry eastward to destroy the important Carr's Bridge over the North Anna.

A few miles farther on, Stoneman "deter- mined to make the most" of his force. He called his commanders together again and "gave them to understand that we had dropped in that region . . . like a shell, and that I intended to burst it in every direction, expecting each piece or fragment to do as much harm . . . as the whole shell, and thus magnify our numbers." On May 3, before dawn, the shell fragments were flying.

Lieutenant Colonel Hasbrock Davis took his Twelfth Illinois under order "to penetrate to the Fredericksburg Railroad, and, if possible, to destroy communications. Should we cross the Virginia Central, I was to make for Wil-liamsburg, said to be in possession of our forces." He burned a bridge on the South Anna and swept into Ashland, which had become a commuters' town for overcrowded Richmond. "Words," he wrote, "cannot describe the astonishment of the inhabitants at our appearance." The raiders ripped up rails, cut telegraph lines, burned twenty wagons, and captured a passing ambulance train. By early evening they were at Hanover Station, burning the trestle, railroad cars, and more wagons.

Gen. David McM. Gregg, U.S.A., and staff.

Lt. Col. Hasbrock Davis, 12th Illinois Cavalry, U.S.A.

At Richmond, less than twenty miles away, a lady afterwards remembered waiting on the President's steps for news: "Mrs. Davis came out and embraced me silently. 'It it dreadful,' I said. 'The enemy are within forty miles of us.' 'Who told you that tale?' she replied. 'They are within three miles of Richmond.' I went down on my knees like a stone." Early next morning President Davis, looking feeble and pale, drove off in his carriage, attended by Colonel Chesnut and Custis Lee with loaded pistols in their holsters, to inspect the city's defenses. "The guns did sound very near," Mrs. Chesnut recorded in her diary, "and

when Mr. Chesnut rode up and told me if Mrs. Davis left Richmond I must go with her, I confess I lost my head. . . . Molly constantly told me, 'Missis, listen to the guns. . . . .'"

Meanwhile, Federal Colonel Hasbrock Davis, pushing southeastward, failed to rout a Confederate blocking force, bypassed it, and, "with nothing to guide me but a common map of the State of Virginia," finished his two-hundred-mile ride at Gloucester Point opposite Yorktown on May 7. Kilpatrick's Second New York performed a similar feat, burning Hungary Station north of Richmond, Meadow Bridge over the Chickahominy, running a train into

78

the river, and picking up 300 prisoners by the time they reached Gloucester. The First New Jersey struck Columbia on the James, and destroyed supplies, bridges, canal boats, and locks while a force under Gregg swept the South Anna clean of bridges. Captain James Robertson, commanding horse artillery, was elated by the lack of Confederate resistance but not with the state of the roads and streams. One river was so swollen that "the carriages were completely submerged, and the horses swimming in harness, dragging the guns after them fully 20 yards." The Confederate War Department was compelled to recall Stuart from the Rappahannock front to deal with these enterprising horsemen.

Stoneman, for his part, since he had no word from Hooker, had swung north by the morning of May 4. "We first began to hear rumors, through Negroes, of the repulse" of "the finest army on the planet," he wrote afterwards. Hooker had "checked" Lee's retreat, was the face-saving description of it by some at the North. "My God!" swore Horace Greeley. "It

Bridge across the Chickahominy River on the Mechanicsville Road, Va.

James Madison Robertson and other officers of the 1st Brigade,
Horse Artillery, U.S.A.

is horrible—horrible; and to think of it, 130,000 magnificent soldiers so cut to pieces by less than 60,000 half-starved ragamuffins."

That morning of the 4th brought Stoneman the fight he expected. A detachment of his Fifth Cavalry, blocking at Shannon's Crossroads, was attacked by over 1000 of the enemy's cavalry. These were "Rooney" Lee's horsemen, who had been waiting for the right moment; and, although the Fifth "checked the attack," Lee said that his Confederates "completely routed them. . . . I could have captured the whole of them but, my horses being tired out by a ride of 50 miles, I would not allow them to follow."

Federal Kentuckian John Buford, who was to save the day at Gettysburg two months later by blunting Lee's advance, was sent by Stoneman to Gordonsville with 650 horsemen to "induce Lee and Hampton to believe that we were going to get out by that way." Another force he sent toward Bowling Green. Buford's "quiet dignity, covering a fiery spirit," was soon to be missed: a disease, exacerbated by exposure and a severe wound, killed him before the year was ended.

Stoneman had his column safe across Raccoon Ford again by May 7. His risk had paid off; the raiders had "exploded" according to plan. All our . . . calculations worked admirably," he reported with satisfaction. It was true as far as it went. But Southerners thought otherwise. He "accomplished nothing of consequence," snorted Jubal Early, "but merely frightened and depredated upon the unarmed country people." This opinion was shared by a *New York Tribune* reporter accompanying the raiders. He wrote bitterly of the depredations: "The carcasses of thousands of horses tainted the poisoned air. . . . Here and there rose, like a grim witness, the blackened shaft that two days before had been the centre of a homestead."

Col. William H. F. "Rooney" Lee, C.S.A.

Gen. John Buford, U.S.A.

It is not improbable that the absence of Stoneman's horsemen cost Hooker the battle of Chancellorsville. Lacking the information they might have furnished him, he had proclaimed, "Lee is in full retreat," as Stonewall Jackson's column marched across his front to fall upon his exposed right flank. The cost of the raid in horses and equipments was enormous: "over 7,000 horses," General Alfred Pleasanton reckoned, "besides the equipment and men left on the road." It had done one thing for the Federal cavalry, however, as Stoneman pointed out, "showing us what we were able to accomplish if we but have the opportunity."

81

Col. Abel Streight, 51st Indiana Infantry, U.S.A.

7

Near Misses and a Hit

DURING THE SPRING of 1863 the Union cavalry blossomed out in the western theater as it had in the east. Several raids of major importance were launched there: some of them successful; others, like Colonel A. D. Streight's, spectacular failures.

Rosecrans's Federals were deadlocked with Bragg's Confederates in middle Tennessee. Streight, impressed by the high Union feeling apparent in the mountains of northern Alabama and eastern Tennessee, submitted a plan to free Rosecrans' forces for movement. He asked for "an independent mounted brigade" which would "draw from the banks of the Cumberland and Ohio the guerrilla bands of Forrest and Morgan and give them employment in their own boasted land of Dixie."

His request was approved, and, on April 7, Streight, in civilian life, an Indianapolis book publisher, received his instructions from Chief-of-Staff James Garfield. From Nashville his command would travel by steamboat, escorted by Alfred Ellett's "horse marines," to Eastport, Mississippi, and join Grenville Dodge's force, which would feint eastward from Corinth. "After having marched long enough with General Dodge," the orders ran, "to create a general impression that you are a part of his expedition, you will push to the south . . . on to western Georgia, and cut the railroads which supply the rebel army by way of Chattanooga (specifically, the bridge across the Etowah River). . . . You will destroy all depots of supplies . . . all manufacturies of guns, ammunition (specifically the Rome, Georgia, foundries)." It was a mission similar to one of the year before, when Ormsby Mitchell had met with failure by dispatching the Andrews raiders from northern Alabama to steal a train between Atlanta and Chattanooga and burn the trestles behind them.

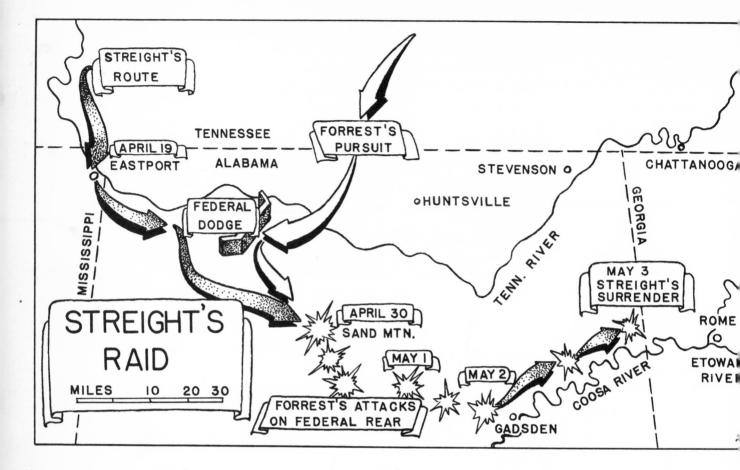

Leaving Dodge's command on April 27, Streight's mule-mounted brigade—mules were considered better than horses for mountain trails—shifted thirty miles to the south and around the demonstration force. Two days later, Streight, "the lively Hoosier," was at the foot of Sand Mountain by dusk. He had destroyed "during the day a large number of wagons laden with provisions," was "now in the midst of devoted Union people," but "could learn nothing of the enemy."

Dodge's demonstration, however, had worked only too well. It had brought Forrest down from Bragg's southern flank, with his "reckless men, who looked to him as their master, their leader, and over whom he had obtained the most complete control." "Shoot at everything blue and keep up the scare," was his order now. Scrambling up the mountain gap in their front, Streight's men formed long enough to check Forrest's impetuous first attack; but they then streamed off eastward for a hundred and fifty miles across northern Alabama to the Georgia line, where on May 3 exhaustion stopped them. "A large portion of my best troops actually went to sleep while lying in line of battle under a severe skirmish fire," their commander reported later.

Under the circumstances Streight's only course was surrender. While talking over the terms, Forrest, whose force at hand equalled only one-third of Streight's, had his cannoneers circle his two guns around a hill until the Fed-

84

eral commander exclaimed: "Name of God! How many guns have you got? There's fifteen I've counted already." He was outraged when he learned how he had been bluffed. "Ah, Colonel," Forrest laughed, "all is fair in love and war, you know." With less than 500 men, Forrest had taken 1466 prisoners. "It was . . . an error to suppose that mules were better suited . . . than horses" for mountain work, Streight decided, when he came to size up the operation.

Another Federal cavalryman, Colonel Benjamin Grierson, raided with complete success this same month. Dogged Grant had been grinding away at Vicksburg's side doors—"The old fool has tried this . . . five times already," was a current comment, "but he's got thirty-seven more plans." Then Admiral David Porter's transports steamed past the Vicksburg batteries to ferry the Union troops across the Mississippi below the fortress; and

Harper's Weekly recorded: "The entire Confederate force in the states bordering on the Mississippi was now being gathered . . . to meet the blows which Grant was preparing. . . . It was at this crisis that Colonel Grierson's raid was undertaken."

"A musician with a profound distrust of horses," after a horse's kick nearly blinded him as a boy, Grierson was "an amateur soldier, his total experience of war packed into eighteen months of training, skirmishing, and some brief but sharp and bitter fighting." His special equipment was "an ordinary Colton's pocket map of the state . . . a small compass . . . a jew's-harp that he probably used more often than either [of the other two]"; but he also had a detailed report of routes, plantations, and supply depots which promised him and his men all the other items they would need.

Pulled out of the Tennessee hills, where he

Federal warehouses and steamboat landing, Chattanooga, Tennessee.

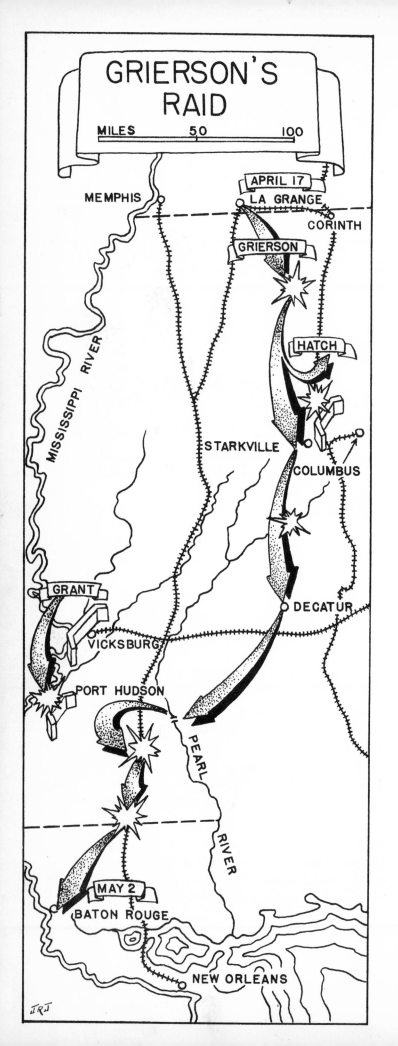

GRIERSON'S RAID

MILES   50   100

MEMPHIS

APRIL 17
LA GRANGE
CORINTH

GRIERSON

HATCH

STARKVILLE

COLUMBUS

GRANT

VICKSBURG

DECATUR

PORT HUDSON

PEARL

RIVER

MISSISSIPPI RIVER

MAY 2
BATON ROUGE

NEW ORLEANS

was chasing guerrillas, he and his brigade of cavalry were ordered south from LaGrange, Tennessee, on April 17 to break off "right and left, cutting both [rail-] roads, destroying the wires, burning provisions, and doing all the mischief they can" to confuse the massing Confederates until Grant could secure his bridgehead on the east bank below Vicksburg.

Vicksburg's alarmed defender, General J. C. Pemberton, soon heard "that several columns of Federal cavalry starting from different points were making inroads into the northern part of Mississippi and that one of them, under Colonel Grierson, was apparently strong enough and bold enough to push on perhaps to the southern limits of the department." Pemberton was helpless to counter the threat, for his cavalry, under General Van Dorn, had been shifted north to aid Braxton Bragg, and without cavalry he had no way of knowing what disaster might occur. He fashioned emergency cavalry out of infantrymen mounted on horses that were "relinquished with the piteous lamentations of the local inhabitants, whose lands were thereby stripped of the means of plowing." He felt compelled "to divert Loring's entire division to the line of the Mobile and Ohio and other railroads, when I most needed the presence of this division nearer Vicksburg."

Grierson rode on his mission virtually unchallenged: only Colonel Edward Hatch's Iowa regiment, which he flung out to one side to cut the railroad at Columbus, Mississippi, was stopped on the 21st by C. R. Barteau's Confederates. Driving the guards from the Pearl River Bridge, Grierson chopped it to pieces and at Decatur "destroyed two warehouses full of commissary stores, several carloads of ammunition . . . the railroad bridges and trestlework." Burning, paroling, and destroying, the raiders worked southward. "Finally, at noon on May 2, the raiders galloped into the streets of Baton Rouge . . . dusty and ragged,"

The 6th and 7th Illinois Cavalry, led by Grierson, rode into Baton Rouge at noon, May 2, 1863.

where they were happy to learn that Federal forces had already taken Port Gibson below Vicksburg, the beginning of the end of that now isolated fortress.

Grierson's highly successful movement—"in sixteen days" it had "traversed 600 miles of hostile territory . . . at a cost of only 27 men" —had been more easily accomplished than the Federal commanders had anticipated. The Rebel strength has been overestimated, he reported. "They have neither the arms nor the resources we have given them credit for." He had brought to light a situation that would encourage raiders for months to come: "The Confederacy was but a hollow shell, strong on the surface by reason of organized armies, but hollow within, and destitute."

87

In the eastern theater, the 9th of June saw what has been called the first true cavalry combat of the war. It enabled the Federals to dispute the reputation for superiority that had thus far been ascribed to the Confederate cavalry. In order to hold a grand review Stuart had assembled 10,000 of his horsemen at Brandy Station. To Hooker, still shaken by his defeat at Chancellorsville, the review looked like the preparation for a grand raid, so he sent Stoneman's successor, General Alfred Pleasonton, with an equal number of Union cavalry, splashing across the Rappahannock to stop it. Pleasonton had been at West Point with Stuart.

The forces of the two old schoolmates collided at Brandy Station. "Acres and acres of horsemen sparkling with sabers, and dotted with brilliant bits of color where their flags danced above them," were "hurled against each other at full speed," as they fought up and down the slopes of a ridge called Fleet-

Gen. Alfred Pleasonton, U.S.A.

Headquarters of General Pleasonton at "Castle Murray," near Auburn, Va.

wood Heights. A Stuart rider watched "the striking phenomenon of gunpowder being ignored almost entirely. Not a man fought dismounted, and there was heard but an occasional pistol shot and but little artillery, for soon after the opening of the fight the contest was so close and the dust so thick that it was impossible to use either without risk to friends."

A Federal horseman told afterwards of how he had wheeled to help a fallen companion "when two fellows put at me. The first one fired at me and missed. Before he could again cock his revolver I succeeded in closing with him. My saber took him just in the neck, and must have cut the jugular. The blood gushed out in a black-looking stream; he gave a horrible yell. . . ." Another trooper remembered: "The cavalry were fighting over and around the guns. . . . There was one rebel, on a splendid horse, who sabered three gunners while I was chasing him. He wheeled in and out— would dart away and then come sweeping back and cut down another man in a manner that seemed almost supernatural. . . . He got off without a scratch."

Adjutant Blackford noticed how "the improvement in the cavalry of the enemy became painfully apparent . . . mainly in their use of dismounted men, and in their horse artillery. . . . They were much better provided with long-range carbines than our cavalry, which gave them an advantage dismounted." Horse sense had become a Federal characteristic. The Giesboro remount depot near Washington had developed into one of the busiest installations of the Union army, processing 6000 horses at a time. After an all-day struggle, the Union

Federal Horse Artilleryman.

Six thousand horses at a time were processed at the Camp Stoneman Cavalry Depot, Giesboro, Md.

89

Terrain such as this, looking down the western slope of Lookout
Mountain, Tenn., into Georgia, prompted Streight to use mules instead
of horses.

The Union cavalry charges under Pleasonton.

Hanover Junction, Pa.: Stuart whipped the Federal cavalry at Hanover, but Lee at Gettysburg lacked the "eyes" of his cavalry.

The First Maine Cavalry fights dismounted.

forces at Brandy Station withdrew across the river. But they carried with them captured dispatches that enabled Pleasonton to report to Hooker that two-thirds of the enemy were at Culpeper preparing to move on Washington.

That move, which, like the one of the previous summer, was actually directed at Maryland and Pennsylvania, was underway in another week. On the 25th the Confederates were at Hagerstown. But now Lee blinded himself, though inadvertently, as Hooker had done before Chancellorsville, by detaching his cavalry for what the impulsive Stuart turned into a wild goose chase. "You had better," ran his ill-defined order, "move over to Fredericktown. You will, however, be able to judge whether you can pass around their army without hindrance . . . and cross the river east of

the mountains." How was Lee to guess that Stuart would take "east" to mean fifteen miles short of Washington, with the result that, as Lee marched northward, the Union army was between him and his cavalry?

That was what Stuart did. It was noon on July 2, the time for decisive cavalry action was long past, and Gettysburg was half finished, when Jeb at last brought his squadrons of jaded riders and lathered horses onto the field. He was credited with having captured a wagon train and close to 1000 prisoners, and had whipped the Federal cavalry at Hanover. But, for want of the information he should have supplied, Lee led a beaten army southward on July 4.

"All of us have some weaknesses," observed a Second Virginia captain. "In his anxiety to do some great thing General Stuart carried his men beyond the range of usefulness." But weary as his men and horses were, he led them into action on the day after his arrival. With four of his brigades and four horse batteries he struck at the right and rear of the Union line. J. B. McIntosh's brigade, supported by George Armstrong Custer's, met him. The combat "swayed from side to side." The action, which began with dismounted skirmish lines and artillery fire, was continued with the brigades of both sides charging in close column of squadrons, with drawn sabers. The Confederates were thrown into confusion and driven back. The batteries resumed their fire, "and at nightfall each side held substantially its original ground."

Capt. Edward A. Flint, 1st Massachusetts Cavalry, U.S.A., and his horse.

Buford's Union cavalry clashes with Stuart's at Boonsboro, Md., as Lee retreats from Gettysburg.

Hon. Clement L. Valladigham of Ohio.

8

Pistols of Gen. John Hunt Morgan.

Morgan Rides North

and Quantrill West

JEB STUART was not the only Southern cavalryman that June of 1863 to stretch a point in interpreting his orders. John Morgan went him one better. Ever fretting in harness to the martinet Bragg, that "cold, austere . . . thorough disciplinarian," Morgan yearned to shake off the boredom of incessant scouting and little other action. At length he asked and was given permission to leave his station on Bragg's right wing in middle Tennessee and raid the acres of the Federal supply depots at Louisville; for Bragg was well aware of Rosecrans' supply problem and of the fact that an average of three Federal infantrymen were required to guard communications against one Confederate cavalryman. "In addition" to striking at Louisville, read Morgan's instructions, "he will . . . break up and destroy the Louisville and Nashville Railroad . . . destroy depots . . . in Kentucky, after which he will return to his present position."

Morgan ferried his command across the Cumberland at Burkesville on July 2, skirmished at Columbia the next day, and rashly attacked Colonel O. H. Moore's Twenty-fifth Michigan in a strong natural position at Green River Bridge. He demanded that the Federals surrender. But Moore replied "that the Fourth of July was no day for me to entertain such a proposition," and after three and a half hours of fighting, Morgan retired with a loss that Moore recorded as over 50 killed and 200 wounded. Though Moore could not have known it, his answer was in tune with the times. That Independence Day marked for the Confederacy the turn in the tide. Vicksburg surrendered that day; Lee was retreating from Gettysburg; and Rosecrans was well along with the process of maneuvering Bragg back on Chattanooga.

Undaunted by the death of his youngest brother, Tom, who fell in a fight with C. S.

95

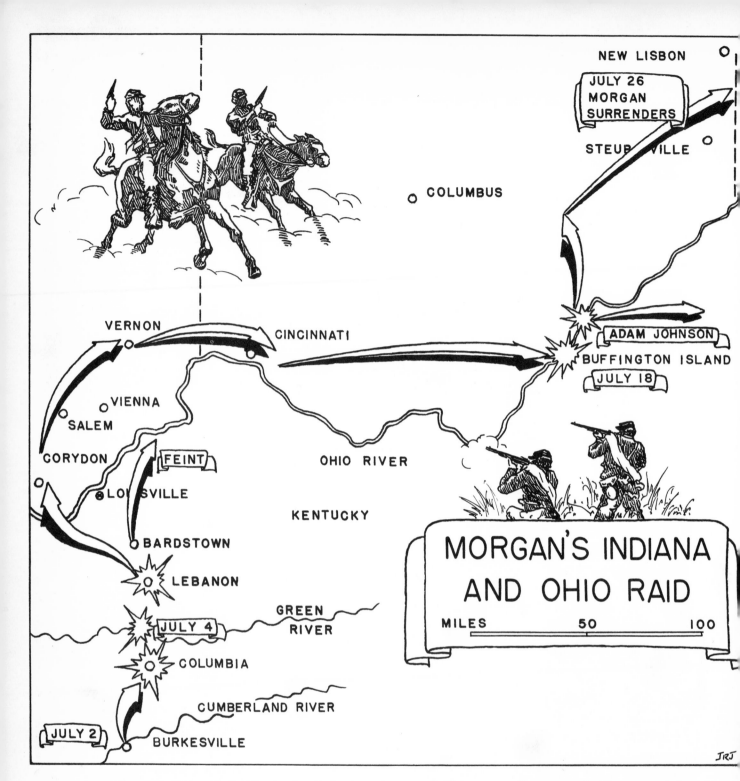

NEW LISBON

JULY 26
MORGAN
SURRENDERS

STEUB_VILLE

COLUMBUS

VERNON   CINCINNATI

ADAM JOHNSON

BUFFINGTON ISLAND

JULY 18

VIENNA

SALEM

CORYDON

FEINT

OHIO RIVER

LOUISVILLE

KENTUCKY

BARDSTOWN

LEBANON

GREEN
RIVER

JULY 4

MORGAN'S INDIANA
AND OHIO RAID

MILES   50   100

COLUMBIA

CUMBERLAND RIVER

JULY 2

BURKESVILLE

JRJ

Hanson's Twentieth Kentucky Infantry at Lebanon, Kentucky, Morgan feinted up-river from Louisville to draw off Federal gunboats, and with his main column rode for Brandenburg, thirty miles down-river from his assigned target. He had stars in his eyes. Rumors of impatient Copperheads in southern Indiana

and Ohio eager for open rebellion gave him dreams of glory, of an army waiting for leadership. Clement L. Vallandigham, leading "ultra-Democrat" in Ohio, "very nearly a Secessionist," and possessed of considerable oratorical power, had so alarmed the administration that he had been tried by a military commission and banished to the Confederate States the previous May.

The probability of stirring up active rebellion north of the Ohio had been endorsed by Morgan's far-roving secret agent, Thomas H. Hines. Hines, who had failed to bring about a mass escape of prisoners-of-war from Camp Douglas at Chicago, had just returned from an undercover trip into Indiana. But, as Morgan headed toward Cincinnati, he found no recruits and, instead, stirred up a hornet's nest in his front and rear. From Cincinnati Major General Burnside, now commanding the Department of Ohio, telegraphed to Washington: "Our mounted force is nearly all occupied in trying to cut him off." Indiana's Governor O. P. Morton pleaded: "Can't you send some

Hon. Oliver P. Morton, Governor of Indiana.

"John Morgan's Highwaymen Sacking a Peaceful Village in the West" read the caption of this bit of propaganda from *Harper's Weekly*. The picture was made from a drawing by Thomas Nast.

Gen. Henry M. Judah, U.S.A.

Hon. William Gannoway Brownlow of Tennessee.

98

Libby Prison. Because Col. A. D. Streight was confined in this Richmond
prison, on charges of inciting slaves to insurrection, Gen. J. H. Morgan
was sent to the Ohio Penitentiary and his head shaven.

PROCLAMATION!

TO THE PEOPLE OF LEBANON!

I am about to leave you. I have endeavored since my entrance in your city to prevent all lawlessness or interference with the rights of any citizens, no matter what his political tenets. If any such interference has occurred, it has been without my knowledge and contrary to my orders, and I now call on any who have been sufferers to come forward and I will repay them.

While I am thus ready to repay all such sufferers, if any, I am equally ready to protect all Southern Rights people in the enjoyment of their opinions, and if any are disturbed in any way whatever, I shall visit the perpetrators with sure and speedy retribution.

JNO. H. MORGAN. Act. Brig. Gen.. C. S. A.

R. A. ALSTON, A. A. G.

cannon? . . . We have nothing here but small arms. The rebels have occupied Corydon. . . . I am organizing militia as fast as possible."

Brigadier General O. B. Willcox, commanding at Indianapolis, forwarded the report of a prisoner taken at Vienna who said, "all he could gather of the intention of the raid . . . was to pass through Indiana and Ohio and join Lee in the east." Brigadier General H. M. Judah packed part of his command on board steamboats at Louisville for the run up-river to Cincinnati. But Morgan had already galloped through Cincinnati's northern outskirts and on along the river, where Federal gunboats steamed parallel to the dust clouds that hung above his column.

Raider J. B. McCreary wrote in his journal: "Like an irresistible avalanche we are sweeping over this country. Man never knows his powers of endurance 'till he tries himself." But one of Morgan's exhausted colonels, Roy S. Cluke, told his commander that he "would give a thousand dollars for an hour's sleep." And

Maj. Daniel McCook, Sr., Paymaster, U.S.V. (mortally wounded, July 19, 1863, at Buffington Island, Ohio.)

99

by July 16 even McCreary had to admit that the avalanche was slowing; "the enemy are now pressing us on all sides, and the woods swarm with militia." For the Federal side, Burnside informed his War Department: "During the past three days . . . [Morgan] has been trying to cross the river . . . but our forces have been harassing" him and "have captured more than half his force."

Twenty miles up-stream from Buffington Island, Morgan again tried to cross and succeeded in putting over Brigadier General A. R. Johnson and 300 men before the enemy gunboats arrived on the scene. He could himself have got across safely, but he preferred to stay with those whom he could not send over.

On July 26, at the end of his tether, near the Pennsylvania line he picked up a captain of militia and asked him if he would accept the Confederates' surrender and release the prisoners on parole: Morgan had released 6000 Federals on parole during the course of the raid. The captain said he would. But things were different when Morgan found himself in the hands of Brigadier General J. M. Shackelford. The General could not forget that "we had followed him for 30 days and nights" and he "regarded his surrender to the militia captain . . . ridiculous."

Since A. D. Streight, whom the Confederates had taken prisoner, had been confined in Libby Prison charged with inciting slaves to insur-

"Tent's eye" view of the Knoxville terrain.

Guarding the bridge across the Holston River, Knoxville.

rection, Morgan was given similar treatment in retaliation. Escorted through a Cincinnati mob to the Ohio Penitentiary, he and his officers were there incarcerated and had their heads shaved like common criminals. A Tennessee Unionist, Parson William G. Brownlow, exulted: "We commenced to celebrate the Fourth of July more than three weeks ago and have been celebrating it ever since. The rebels have gone up the ropes at Tullahoma, Lee has been run out of Pennsylvania, and I don't know what will become of that consecrated, lying horse thief, John Morgan."

An Illinois private, disgusted with the complacency that prevailed in his home state, wrote to his wife: "We learn that Morgan and

Col. Dick Morgan

Capt. Charlton H. Morgan

Confederate Brigadier Basil Duke, Morgan's brother-in-law and second in command, fought off Federals pursuing the Morgan raiders for hours before being overwhelmed in Ohio. Michigan and Indiana cavalry swept up 700 exhausted Confederate prisoners which included two of Morgan's brothers, Col. Dick Morgan and Capt. Charlton H. Morgan. The capture was Charlton Morgan's third.

102

A Federal cavalryman.

his band had rather poor luck in Indiana and Ohio. I wish they had ventured over into Illinois and done a little of their stealing and burning." The raid had, indeed, greatly stimulated the war spirit in the states it had traversed. It must have been cold comfort to Morgan that his exploit's one distinction was its having reached the northernmost point of any organized Confederate Army effort.

A "diversion in favor of General Morgan," which was launched from Knoxville by Major General Simon Buckner, who commanded the Confederate Department of East Tennessee, was equally unsuccessful. Led by Colonel John S. Scott, the "objects of the expedition were to cut the enemy's communications; to destroy their trains and supplies; to capture horses, mules, and arms; to send out cattle." But Scott's riders found that they had diverted more than they could handle when "the concentration by rail of the enemy's force in greatly superior numbers converted . . . success into partial disaster."

Col. William Clark Quantrill, C.S.A.

Hon. James H. Lane of Kansas.

The bitterness generated by such raids as Morgan's, however, was but a pale reflection of the ferocity of the Kansas-Missouri border warfare. Pro-slavery Missourians and Abolitionist Kansans had fought for a decade before the war, with massacre and counter-massacre, in which John "Pottawatomie" Brown had a bloody role before he was stopped at Harper's Ferry. Shortly before the war, a skinny teenager named William Clark Quantrill moved to Kansas from Ohio to teach school a few miles from the spot where Brown's raiders had hacked the arms off a pro-slaver's sons in 1855. Stimulated by this background of partisan hatreds, Quantrill decided that the Missourians' wrongs were the greater and applied for a Confederate commission as an independent cavalry leader when the war began. Many Missourians who intended to fight for the protection of their families did the same thing.

The Union side found a leader in James H. Lane, a former lieutenant governor of Indiana

103

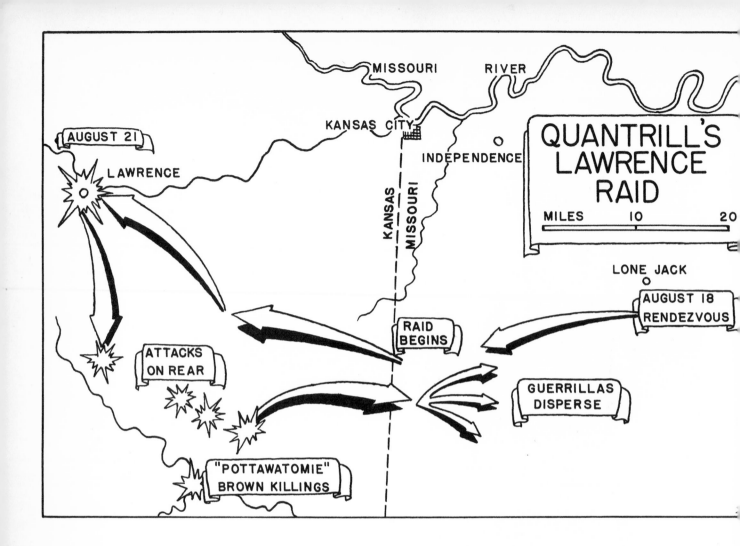

and a rabid Abolitionist. It was said of his oratory that "he talked like none of the rest. None of the others had that husky, rasping, blood-curdling whisper, or could shriek 'Great God' on the same day with him." Operating from Lawrence, Kansas, the center of Abolitionist sentiment, his raiders ravaged rural Missouri and burned the towns of Osceola, Nevada, and Butler. His performances, like Morgan's, injured his own cause. As early as December 1861, General H. W. Halleck had notified the War Department: "The conduct of the forces under Lane and [Dr. Charles] Jennison has done more for the enemy in this State than could have been accomplished by 20,000 of his own army. I receive almost daily complaint of outrages." By the middle of 1863,

when the situation had become intolerable in Missouri, Quantrill held a colonel's commission in the Confederate Army and was a veteran of the battle of Wilson's Creek and numerous smaller actions, in many of which he had co-operated with Sterling Price and his cavalry leaders, Marmaduke and Jo Shelby.

Major General J. M. Schofield, at that time commanding the Department of Missouri, wrote directly to President Lincoln near the summer's end, describing his efforts to eradicate guerrilla warfare from the state. "Upon the representation of General Ewing and others familiar with the facts," he had become "satisfied that there could be no cure . . . short of the removal from those counties of all slaves entitled to their freedom, and of the families

Gen. John S. Marmaduke, C.S.A.

of all men known to belong to these [guerrilla] bands, and others . . . known to sympathize with them."

Almost immediately after it became known that such a policy had been adopted, Quantrill assembled about 300 of his men secretly near the Kansas line and marched on Lawrence. Using a prepared black list, his raiders, among whom were the future outlaws Cole Younger and Frank James, struck savagely at dawn on August 21. They burned most of the town and killed nearly 200 men and boys. Lane escaped them by hiding in a cornfield. The house of the first Kansas governor, Dr. Charles Robinson, whom Quantrill respected, afforded asylum to General George Deitzler of the Kansas volunteers.

The raiders had to fight their way back to Missouri, but they covered the sixty miles by the following morning and dispersed into the

A soldier's version of Quantrill's bloody raid on Lawrence, Kan.

Sam Hildebrand, one of Quantrill's riders.

Gen. Thomas Ewing, U.S.A.

Order No. 11—"All persons . . . hereby ordered to be removed . . . out of this district."

Blacksmithing near Tipton on the Missouri Prairie.

hills south of Independence. General Thomas Ewing, commander of the Department of the Border, through whose territory Quantrill had moved, retaliated with his notorious Depopulation Order Number 11. It read in part: "All persons [of the three border counties] . . . are hereby ordered to be removed . . . out of this district."

But it was Quantrill who drew the last blood. Schofield notified the War Department in October that: "General [James G.] Blunt's escort was surprised by Quantrill, south of Fort Scott," where, according to Quantrill, they "fled in the wildest confusion," adding that "we soon closed up . . . making fearful havoc" in a "chase of about four miles, only leaving about 40 of them alive."

A murderer several times over, both before and during the war, Quantrill came to a well-deserved end early in 1865. On a raid into Kentucky with thirty-three men, he was surprised by Federal irregulars, who defeated and mortally wounded him. He died in a Louisville hospital some weeks later, a disgrace to the government that had given him a commission. It was under him that the notorious bandit Jesse James received his training in lawlessness and cruelty.

107

Gen. Joseph Wheeler, C.S.A.

Confederate lance or guidon pennant.

Once around Rosecrans

WHEN BRAGG was forced out of middle Tennessee in the summer of 1863, the action culminated in the September battle of Chickamauga close to the southern outskirts of Chattanooga. The result was a beaten Federal army bottled up in Chattanooga by Bragg's victorious troops, its back to the Tennessee River. Siege, plus starvation, could make the place a Vicksburg for Rosecrans. It was only necessary to cut off his supply lines to the north.

Joe Wheeler, whose "meteoric rise," it has been said, "seems due, not so much to brilliance, as to his ability to take an order and then stay on the job night and day," was the man to make the cut. In order to give him sufficient horsemen Bragg assigned Forrest's men to him. "You will without delay turn over the troops of your command . . . to Major General Wheeler," ran the curt order.

Forrest, who feared a superior no more than he did the enemy, burst raging into Bragg's tent, refused his proffered hand, and proceeded to light into his commander: "You commenced your cowardly . . . persecution after Shiloh . . . because I reported to Richmond facts, while you reported damned lies. You robbed me of my command . . . that I armed and equipped from the enemies. . . . You are a coward and a damned scoundrel. . . . You may as well not issue any more orders to me, for I will not obey them." And he stomped off to Montgomery to interview Jefferson Davis, who gave him an independent command.

"Forrest should have been the commander," in the opinion of a Wheeler biographer, "not only because he was better fitted for this type of work, but for the additional reason that Wheeler's troops apparently showed no resentment at being commanded by Forrest while

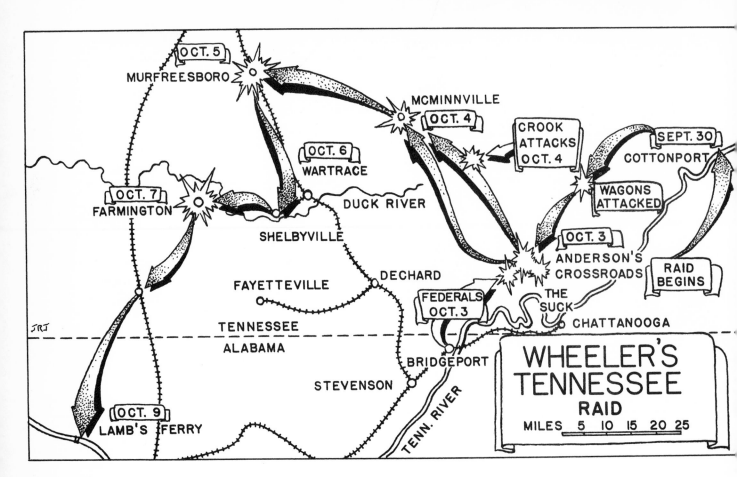

WHEELER'S TENNESSEE RAID

the same could not be said in reverse order."
Wheeler discovered, moreover, that Forrest's
men were poorly armed, their supply of ammunition small. They were very weary, and
their horses were "in horrible condition, having been marched continuously for three days
and nights without removing saddles."

On September 30, however, Wheeler led a
force of 4000 troopers into the Tennessee River
at Cottonport, up-stream from Chattanooga.
"Then the line swung down the stream across
the silvery surface," one participant remembered, "like the windings of a huge dark
serpent." They burned thirty-two wagons in
Sequatchie Valley on October 3, got into an

unexpected cavalry fight at Anderson's Crossroads, and were astonished to see, extending
for ten miles along the mountain toward Jasper, "hundreds of large Federal wagons . . .
with their big white covers on them, like so
many African elephants, solemn in their stately
grandeur. . . . It had rained the night before
and left the roads so slippery that the wagons
could not go over the steep mountain pass. . . .
They had been rushed up there by the team-
sters and abandoned. Some had escaped by
cutting loose the mules and mounting them."

Two brigades of Federal cavalry had to be
driven off before the size of this capture could
be fully appreciated. It was then discovered to

Gen. George Crook, U.S.A.

amount to 750 wagons, 2600 fat mules, and 1200 prisoners. The wagons, or most of them, were loaded with rations. The captors spent the next eight hours burning wagons and sabering mules. "I was particularly struck with the fine harness that had been stripped from the mules," wrote a Fourth Tennessee trooper. "It lay chin deep over ten acres of ground." So "full of plunder" were the soldiers that fighting, it was said, had "gone out of their minds."

Now Wheeler's problem was to get away before the alarmed Federals could close in upon him. When Federal Brigadier General Crook galloped into Sequatchie Valley with two brigades, he found that Wheeler had split

Gen. Joe Wheeler, driving off two brigades of Union cavalry, captures a supply train of 750 wagons near Jasper, Tenn., October 3, 1863.

111

Ripped up by raiders, a railroad track near Murfreesboro, Tenn., is repaired for use again.

112

his force into two columns and decamped for McMinnville, where Wheeler's men captured the 400-man garrison and stores that were said to include "a full suit of clothing for every man in Rosecrans' army." Swinging around Murfreesboro, Wheeler destroyed the bridge over Stones River and three miles of track. During the following day he burned all the trestles as far as Wartrace, blew up a train, and took Shelbyville. Federal Major General Gordon Granger had telegraphed the commander at Wartrace: "Move your troops at once to Duck River bridge and hold that point until every man is sacrificed." But the Wartrace garrison had already left.

Gen. Robert B. Mitchell, U.S.A.

Fortified bridge at Nashville on the Louisville and Nashville Railroad.

Gen. William S. Rosecrans, U.S.A.

A host of Union troops swarmed in to trap the raiders at Farmington, Tennessee. A division of infantry and one of cavalry had arrived there when Wheeler, just in time, placed five regiments of Martin's command in position. "We fought them with great warmth for twenty minutes," Wheeler commented. So his command managed to scramble past. "The enemy should have destroyed us at Farmington," said Confederate George Guild, for the raiders "were flushed with booty, and the Federals were smarting under their heavy losses."

The last day of the raid saw Wheeler's troopers streaming toward the safety that lay beyond fordable Muscle Shoals on the Tennessee. Wheeler's action looked like "a rout" to Federal Brigadier General D. S. Stanley, cavalry chief for the Department of the Cumberland: "His command were running all day for the river, every man for himself, and hats,

Pvt. Achille Ferris, Co. H, 8th Texas Cavalry, c.s.a. (Terry's Texas Rangers)

Terry's Texas Rangers rode with Wheeler.

canteens, coats, guns and broken-down horses were strewn along the whole route." Wheeler had barely escaped disaster, and he could only guess at the total of his accomplishment, some of which was indirect. Some of his pursuers were suffering from an exhaustion equal to that of his own men. "My command is . . . badly used up," reported Federal General Robert Mitchell. "Hard marches, scarcity of shoes . . . and miserable, worthless saddles . . . have ruined many of the horses." But Wheeler had the satisfaction of learning that the Union troops in Chattanooga were now on quarter rations. Starving soldiers, it was said, were following the forage wagons in the hope of picking up stray ears of corn.

Grant was detailed to superintend the situation. Hooker was hurried from the Army of the Potomac to secure a line through which reinforcements and supplies could be brought into the beleaguered town. By early October he was on the north bank of the Tennessee at Stevenson, Alabama. To cover "the short reach of 26 miles of railroad or 28 miles of road . . .

Col. Henry M. Ashby, 2nd Tennessee Cavalry, C.S.A.

was now all that was necessary. But Rosecrans must first secure . . . the route, rebuild the bridge across the Tennessee, and the trestle at Whiteside . . . which would take longer than his stock [of provisions] would last."

Rosecrans ordered "small, flat-bottomed steamers" to get rations up to within reach of Chattanooga until the railroad was running. But the river in the gorge, "the Suck," through Raccoon Mountain, was "very rapid and narrow," noted a dubious engineer, "and navigating up-stream" could only be done with windlass and shore-lines. On October 5 the boat-builder's journal recorded, "General Hooker was over . . . and examined the little

The viaduct on the Chattanooga Railroad, Tennessee, between Shellmound Station and Whiteside.

Falling Water Bridge on the Nashville and Chattanooga Railroad.

scow," and ordered work to be "crowded on it as fast as possible. October 16 . . . the planking nearly all on. . . . 24th: the steamer launched safely. . . . On the 29th she made her first trip . . . 34,000 rations. . . . In Chattanooga there were but four boxes of hard bread left. . . . The orderly reported that the news went through the camps faster than his horse. 'The cracker line open! Full rations, boys!'"

In the last week of November, Grant ("When that old cuss is around, there is sure to be a big fight somewhere.") saw his troops drive Bragg's Confederates off Missionary Ridge.

Windlass and shore lines were required to get a ration boat for the Union through "The Suck" in the Raccoon Mountain gorge near Chattanooga.

Gen. Judson Kilpatrick, U.S.A.

10

"That Crazy Fool" Kilpatrick

and George Custer

URING THE MONTHS that followed the battle of Gettysburg, Lee had gradually withdrawn his army until, early in October, it lay behind the Rapidan, with the Army of the Potomac facing it in a position around Culpeper. Thinking that he saw a chance of getting between the Union army and Washington, Lee began on the 9th a series of maneuvers intended to envelop the Federal right flank. It failed to force Meade to fight a battle facing to the rear, as it was intended to do, although it did drive him back to the positions McDowell's army had occupied before First Manassas. The one bright episode for Southerners in this so-called "Bristoe campaign" was contributed by Stuart's cavalrymen.

Encountering Judson Kilpatrick's Federal cavalry along Broad Run on October 19, Stuart set a trap for him. With Fitz Lee's squadrons concealed on the right of the road, Stuart simulated a retreat. Kilpatrick sent a brigade in hot pursuit. The trap was sprung;

the Blue horsemen broke; and the "frantic steeplechase," over the five miles from Buckland Mills to Broad Run, that resulted was called ever after by the Confederates the "Buckland Races." Kilpatrick himself didn't stop until he was behind the Union infantry.

Although he had done creditable work at Gettysburg, Kilpatrick, "the boy general," had made few friends among Meade's subordinates. One of them characterized him as "a frothy braggart, without brains and not over-stocked with desire to fall on the field . . ." a man who got "all his reputation by newspapers and political influence." He did, indeed, love the showy side of military life, and the "Kilpatrick hat," with its brim turned up on the left and down on the right, was prescribed for his Third Cavalry Division. "Kill-cavalry," his troopers called him, from the recklessness with which he led them and wore out both men and horses. Early in 1864 he came up with the idea of a raid so bold that its very audacity appears to

119

Kilpatrick figured he could empty Belle Isle (in the James River at
Richmond) of imprisoned Federals.

have commended it to his superiors. He was
directed to go to Washington and submit to
the President a plan "to accomplish the
double purpose of distributing the President's
amnesty proclamation to the rebel command
. . . and attempt to release our prisoners at
Richmond."

Belle Isle, prisoner-of-war camp in the James
River at Richmond, had become overcrowded
since General Halleck's order in May 1863,
had slowed exchanges, and Kilpatrick figured
that he could empty it. Meade doubted the
feasibility of the plan and conferred with
Pleasonton, who had even more doubts. "When
the Stoneman raid was made last year,"
Pleasonton pointed out, "General Lee's army
was closely engaged . . . and the country was
clear." It was not so at this time.

President Lincoln, however, thought that
the plan would work. Accordingly, Kilpatrick's

121

division was reinforced with picked troops from all the other divisions of the cavalry corps. A great effort was made to keep the preparations secret, for Meade considered success possible only by a rapid and secret movement. But unfortunately, as a staff officer soon found out, "a secret expedition with us is got up like a picnic, with everybody blabbing and yelping. . . . Kilpatrick is sent for by the President: oh, ah! everybody knows it at once; he is a cavalry officer; it must be a raid. All Willards chatters of it."

"To create a diversion in your favor," Kilpatrick was told, "a powerful expedition has been organized and will be in full movement tomorrow . . . to operate toward the left flank of the enemy in the direction of Charlottesville. . . . This operation will be followed by other movements." As Theodore Lyman explained it: "All this, you see, was on our right. . . . Kilpatrick . . . on our extreme left . . . drew a straight bead on Richmond."

On Sunday night, February 28, 1864, Kilpatrick, at the head of 3500 men, slipped out of the Culpeper country. He was blessed with weather that a literary-minded signal officer described: "Myriads of stars twinkled in heaven, looking at us as if in wonder why we

Culpeper, Va.: "Myriads of stars twinkled" overhead when Kilpatrick's cavalry slipped away for Richmond.

122

Kilpatrick's troopers take the road to Richmond.

should break the laws of God and wander at night instead of seeking repose and sleep. The moon threw its silvery light upon Rapidan waters when we forded it, and it seemed as if the Almighty Judge was looking silently upon our doings."

In command of the advance party rode one-legged Colonel Ulric Dahlgren, son of Rear Admiral John Dahlgren, inventor of the famous Dahlgren gun. His task was "to move rapidly forward by way of Spotsylvania Court House . . . to a point above Goochland on the James River, cross the river, move down the opposite bank, and, if possible, be in position to seize the main bridge that led to Richmond at 10 o'clock, Tuesday, March 1."

Kilpatrick's main column reached Beaver Dam Station on the Virginia Central Railroad by midday on Monday, February 29. His scouts had done such a thorough job of cutting the telegraph wires in front of him that Confederate Brigadier General P. M. B. Young was

123

Discussing the probabilities of the next move.

astonished when he found that the raiders had slipped through his fingers. "The first intimation that I had of the move was about 11 a.m. on the 1st day by a citizen who had been run from his house by the second column, the first column having passed in the night without waking anyone. . . . I thought it must be a false alarm." Kilpatrick was forty miles to the south before Young could act.

On Monday night, after tearing up the Virginia Central track, Kilpatrick bivouacked briefly nine miles short of the South Anna. His men were in the saddle again by midnight, however. He had intended to ride through Richmond and be in possession of the north end of Mayo's Bridge by ten the next morning. But his guide led the column toward Ashland and into the Confederate pickets. Drawing back, he crossed the South Anna, chose another route, and advanced against scattering resistance until, within a mile of Richmond, he was confronted by a considerable force of infantry and artillery under the command of Robert E. Lee's son Custis.

Col. Ulric Dahlgren, U.S.A.

Gen. Pierce M. B. Young, C.S.A.

124

Believing that this opposition was only militia, he formed his troops, attacked, and was forcing the enemy back slightly when he discovered that they were rapidly receiving reinforcements not only of infantry but artillery. "Feeling confident that Dahlgren had failed to cross the river . . . I reluctantly withdrew . . . crossed the Meadow Bridge over the Chickahominy and . . . went into camp near Mechanicsville."

Meanwhile Dahlgren, with his 500 troopers, had swept into Fredericks Hall Station at 11 a.m. on the 29th and captured a court-martial that was in session there. But the station itself was so heavily garrisoned that he rode around it and was across the South Anna before midnight. It began to rain. Fifty of his men became separated from the column and only caught up with it at dawn, when it was nearing the James. He had now to cross not only the river but the Kanawha Canal, which ran along its northern bank.

He detached a hundred of his Second New Yorkers and sent them down the northern bank on an errand of destruction. "He divided the torpedoes," reported the commander of this detachment, "giving me one box, some turpentine and oakum. Along the canal I destroyed six flourishing grist mills filled with grain and flour, one sawmill, six canal boats loaded with grain, the barn (also well filled) on Secretary Seddon's plantation, coal works

at Manakin's Ferry, and Morgan's Lock just above."

Dahlgren pressed forward. But he had no luck in finding a passage across the river. As the Richmond *Daily Examiner* reported it: "The victim of their brutal wrath was a boy named Martin, the property of Mr. David Meems, of Goochland. It appears that the Negro was impressed as a pilot, and had informed the Yankees that they could cross the river at Jude's Ferry, about two miles from Dover Mills. The river was, however, fuller than usual." A Richmond woman retold the story as she had it from a prisoner: "He saw them hang the Negro who had misled them, unintentionally in all probability. He saw Dahlgren give a part of his bridle to hang

Ruins of a mill on the James River and Kanawha Canal. Six grist mills, a saw mill, and six canal boats loaded with grain were destroyed by Kilpatrick.

125

him." The troopers of the Second New York, hurrying back to the river road after their work of destruction along the canal, passed the body of the Negro swinging from a tree. They were eight miles from Richmond when they caught up with Dahlgren.

Dahlgren halted for an hour to give his men and horses a much needed rest. He had abandoned the project of seizing the Mayo Bridge. He could hear the artillery of Kilpatrick's fight to the north. He had captured three men of the hastily mobilized City Battalion. "About five miles from the city," said a Federal officer, "we were met by a volley from the woods. At first there was some wavering. . . . The only way we had of advancing was to charge over their line of skirmishers." "It was pouring rain, cold and pitch dark," a

Gen. Richard L. T. Beale, C.S.A.

126

Confederate War Department clerk, who was called out for the defense, told a friend afterwards. "Still, we were near enough to hear their words of command."

Groping through the rest of that day and into the following night in an attempt to rejoin Kilpatrick, Dahlgren stumbled into a Confederate force at Hungary Station, losing half his column in the confusion and darkness. At daylight another enemy force stalled him at Hanover Court House. More of them were awaiting him on the South Anna, he gathered; so he headed east, for White House Landing, having heard that Kilpatrick had gone that way with the main body. "Every few minutes [his] advance guard would have a skirmish with some of the enemy, till finally, about eight miles from Tunstall's Station, the enemy . . . opposed our further passage." Dahlgren managed to slip his command past them. But a detachment of Colonel R. L. T. Beale's Ninth Virginia ambushed him at midnight near King and Queen Court House, and the lieutenant in command reported: "The colonel [Dahlgren] commanding was killed at the first fire. . . . They then retreated in great confusion." One hundred and thirty-five Federal surrendered to a prisoner they had taken a short time before.

Ulric Dahlgren was almost fanatical in his devotion to the Union cause. Papers of the most dreadful purport were said to have been found upon his body, written in his own hand and signed with his name. "We hope to release the prisoners on Belle Island first," one read, "and having seen them fairly started, we will cross the James River into Richmond, destroying the bridges after us and exhorting the released prisoners to destroy and burn the hateful city . . . and not allow the rebel leader Davis and his traitorous crew to escape." "The city must be destroyed," ran another, "and Jeff Davis and his cabinet killed."

These papers were hurried to Richmond, and General Robert E. Lee sent a personal letter through the lines to General George Meade: "I have the honor to enclose photographic copies of the papers. . . . I beg leave to inquire whether the instructions . . . were authorized by the United States government?"

Of course they were not authorized. But a Richmond girl noted: "Now that Dahlgren has failed to carry out his orders, the Yankees disown them; they disavow it all. He was not sent here to murder us all, hang the President, and burn the town. There is the notebook, however, at the Executive office, with the orders to hang and burn." Dahlgren's body robbed of all valuables and its artificial leg received what the *Examiner* said it deserved, "a dog's burial, without coffin, pall or service." Few in Richmond, probably thought it strange that, if Dahlgren had indeed signed those orders, he should have misspelled his own name—Dahlgren for Dahlgren—in doing so. Without doubt, a few more deplored the fact that one of the Colonel's little fingers had been cut off to facilitate the theft of a ring. This, in the North, was expanded into a charge that the body had been mutilated.

In the Northern army the more jealous of Kilpatrick's fellow officers read with sardonic amusement in his official report: "If Colonel Dahlgren had not failed in crossing the river . . . or had the enemy at Bottom's Bridge been forced to remain at that point . . . I should have entered the rebel capital. . . . The expedition failed in its great object." In the fresh New York papers that came in on the flag-of-truce boats, Richmond people were pleased to read: "They are down on Kilpatrick for his miserable failure before Richmond." A Federal staff officer wrote to his wife: "Now all that cavalry must be carried back in steamers, like a parcel of old women going to market." Still more pointed was General M.

The canal at Richmond.

T. McMahon's comment: "Aside from our losses in men . . . the result . . . was to disable for the time being 3,000 or 4,000 of the very flower of our cavalry."

Meanwhile the diversion for Kilpatrick's attempt had been more successful. The day before the raid started: "on Saturday [Feb. 27] at early morn," wrote Theodore Lyman, "Uncle John Sedgewick suddenly picked up his little traps and marched with his corps through Culpeper and out towards Madison Court House, away on our right flank." This was to draw the Confederate cavalry westward, away from Kilpatrick's route. To magnify this feint General George Custer was called back from the beginning of his honeymoon at Washington to lead a 1500-man raid into Albemarle County in an attempt to destroy the Lynchburg Railroad Bridge over the Rivanna, near Charlottesville. "I found myself in a few hours on the extreme wing of the Army of the Potomac," his bride lamented, "in an isolated Virginia farm house, finishing my honeymoon alone."

127

Gen. George Custer, U.S.A.

Mill at Stanardsville, Va., burned by Custer's Cavalry, March 1, 1864.

Leaving his Pony Mountain camp on Sunday afternoon, the 28th, the bridegroom had ridden west to Madison Court House by nightfall. A trooper grumbled, "There goes taps, and before we get a mouthful to eat . . . Old Curley will hike us out." His estimate was close, for Custer had his column moving before two in the morning.

"Old Curley" was half a misnomer. The bean-pole Ohioan was only twenty-five when he ended the war as a major general. But his mane of yellow hair was curly enough. Strangers were tempted to laugh also at the yards of gold braid that decorated Custer's favorite uniform of black velvet. "This officer is one of the funniest looking human beings you ever saw," observed one of Meade's officers, "and looks like a circus rider gone mad." But Custer was a hell-for-leather cavalryman. "Fighting for fun is rare. . . . Custer and some others attacked whenever they got a chance, and of their own accord."

Galloping into Stanardsville shortly after daylight, he sent the enemy pickets flying and

Advance of Custer's cavalry brigade.

Gen. George Meade, U.S.A.

learned from prisoners that Fitz Lee's cavalry was recruiting and foraging near Charlottesville. Cautious now, he sighted the Southerner's pickets six miles out. But they fired quick shots and scurried back to the town; and the Confederate commander there telegraphed hastily to his superior at Lynchburg: "Enemy's cavalry three miles from town. Can you send me any assistance? I want infantry." A startled Brigadier General Nichols at Lynchburg relayed the message to Richmond, adding, "I have telegraphed . . . that I cannot"; and Charlottesville's veteran commander, armless since Chancellorsville, could only shout for citizens to turn out with their guns, for he had no soldiers.

Custer, however, concentrated on the accomplishment of his mission. "We succeeded," he wrote, "in driving the enemy . . . until we reached a point about two miles beyond the Rivanna River, and within three miles of Charlottesville. Here I discovered a superior force of the enemy's cavalry, supported by four batteries of artilley. . . . To satisfy myself

129

Gen. Francis T. Nichols, C.S.A.

concerning the enemy's strength and position I ordered Captain Ash, of the 5th U. S. Cavalry . . . to charge the enemy's right flank."

The enemy was Stuart's horse artillery, and Confederate Captain M. N. Moorman discovered the Federal riders among his tents before he could sound an alarm. "Finding it impossible to get out of camp unless some check could be given, I opened fire with a portion of the guns of each battery, while the drivers and remaining cannoneers caught and hitched up the horses, all of which were running loose. As fast as a carriage was horsed it was moved off. . . . The enemy by this time had pressed back through camp the line of skirmishers . . . which I had deployed to my front."

While Ash's detachment burned the camp and several abandoned caissons, the Federal right, a Confederate artilleryman said, "made a charge just in time to receive and mistake

General Custer, surrounded by his staff, talks with Captain Ash and prisoners.

the explosion of one of Captain Chew's caissons for the reopening of our guns. . . . Each column, mistaking the other for his enemy, fired into the other"; the Confederates rallied and pushed both columns back toward the river.

Ash's men were not impressed by the damage done them in the fight: "4 skillets, 2 campkettles, 4 water-buckets." But Custer was able to report: "After recrossing the Rivanna I burned the bridge over that stream" and "three large flour mills filled with grain and flour." Homeward bound now, the raiders gleaned 500 horses from the countryside before dusk, when they made a halt a few miles short of Stanardsville. A blinding rainstorm, however, caused a third of the command to continue on in the darkness, and at dawn Custer's weakened column collided with "quite a large body of cavalry. . . . The enemy charged our advance, drove them in rapidly to the main body."

Pulling his main body into a ravine, Custer waited. In another moment his retreating advance guard was followed by gray-coated horsemen who came "pouring out of the woods in large numbers. . . . General Custer," as a junior officer wrote proudly, "ordered a charge of his entire force . . . moving forward in magnificent style . . . upon the enemy, driving them back in confusion. We captured about half a dozen prisoners, and learned from them that we were fighting General Stuart with two brigades of cavalry."

Col. G. W. Custis Lee, C.S.A.

Custer's artillery discouraged a Confederate rally this time. Stuart's men gathered again to oppose Custer when he feinted toward Burton's Ford on the Rapidan. But "before he could detect my movement," Custer "faced . . . about and moved rapidly to Bank's Ford at which point I crossed without molestation." He and his men ate supper near Madison Court House.

More fortunate than Kilpatrick, Custer could write: "My command returned to its camp without having suffered the loss of a man." He had, to be sure, failed to destroy the railroad bridge, but Pleasonton was pleased with the total result and expressed his "entire satisfaction . . . at the prompt manner in which the duties assigned to you have been performed."

Burning bridge over the Rivanna River.

131

Gen. Phil Sheridan, U.S.A.

Once around Lee

Pleasonton's cavalry deployed as skirmishers move forward.

IF STONEMAN's 1863 raid behind Lee's army showed the Federal cavalry its possibilities, Sheridan's raid a year later convinced both North and South that the blue-coated horsemen, properly handled, had no superiors. During the previous year Pleasonton had much increased the efficiency of this branch of the service. He had consolidated into a corps of three divisions a force that formerly had been composed of disconnected regiments and brigades. But he had strained his relations with Meade in doing so.

That March Colonel Theodore Lyman wrote home optimistically about the shake-up that followed Grant's appointment to the highest command. "For chief of cavalry we are to have a General Sheridan, from the West. He is, I believe, on his way. If he is an able officer, he will find no difficulty in pushing along this arm, several degrees." On being introduced to General Philip H. Sheridan, he found him "a small, broad-shouldered, squat man, with black hair and a square head. He is of Irish parents, but looks very like a Piedmontese."

Assuming command on April 6, 1864, Sheridan saw no reason why he should not keep the relieved Pleasonton's subordinate commanders—"I never had reason to regret it"—and plunged into the job of righting cavalry wrongs. But he did see reasons for changing Pleasonton's methods of using the cavalry. He found "the horses thin and very much worn down by excessive . . . picket duty . . . establishment of cordons . . . with hardly a mounted Confederate confronting it at any point. . . . I took in this situation and determined to remedy it if possible."

Realizing that "the effectiveness of my command rested mainly on the strength of its horses," Sheridan spent his first month putting the mounts in shape for the impending summer campaigns. With supplies and remounts

133

pouring in by way of Belle Plain, ten miles east of Fredericksburg, he established policies that permitted necessary rest, as the Confederates were doing, husbanding the strength of his horses by keeping them in the rear. This done, he visited General Meade, his new commander, to "give him my idea of what cavalry should do, the main purport of which was that it ought to be kept concentrated to fight the enemy's cavalry. . . . My proposition seemed to stagger General Meade not a little."

"Meade would hardly listen to my proposition . . . deemed cavalry fit for little more than guard and picket duty"; and when Grant moved Meade's army across the Rapidan to fight the battles of the Wilderness and Spotsylvania, Meade continued to issue personal orders directly to the cavalry units. Sheridan, deeply roiled, argued with Meade that he could whip Stuart if only he would let him; but since Meade insisted on giving the cavalry

directions without consulting him, then Meade could command the cavalry corps himself.

An indignant Meade repeated these remarks to Grant. But Grant said: "Then let him go out and do it." Meade therefore issued immediate orders to "proceed against the enemy's cavalry, and when your supplies are exhausted, proceed . . . to the James River, there communicating with General Butler, procuring supplies and return to this army."

With his divisions under the command of David Gregg, James Wilson, and Wesley Merritt, Sheridan left the Fredericksburg country on May 9 and swung around Lee's right flank. His 10,000 horsemen, massed on a single road, formed a column thirteen miles long. But he preferred that to using a number of parallel roads, for "an engagement was at all times imminent, hence it was specially necessary to keep the whole force well together."

134

Gen. Pleasonton was pictured by a Northern artist at the head of a blue-coated column on the march in a snow storm.

Troopers of Sheridan water their horses at Belle Plain.

135

Detachment of 1st U.S. Cavalry, Brandy Station, Va.

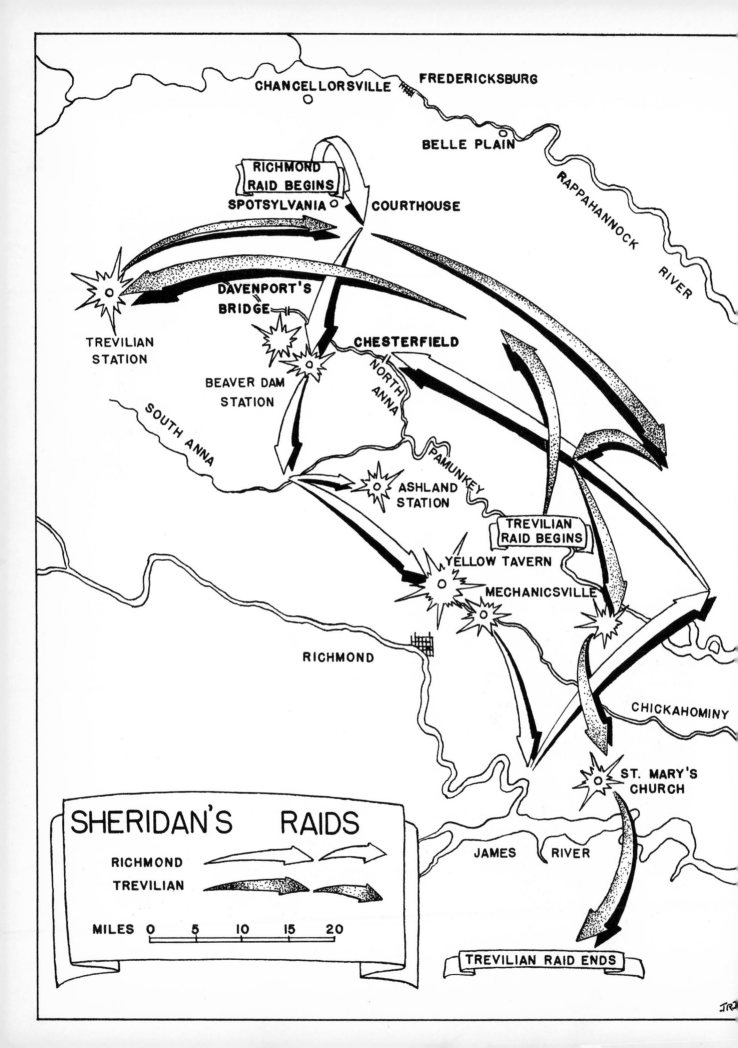

CHANCELLORSVILLE   FREDERICKSBURG

BELLE PLAIN

RAPPAHANNOCK RIVER

RICHMOND
RAID BEGINS

SPOTSYLVANIA   COURTHOUSE

DAVENPORT'S
BRIDGE

TREVILIAN
STATION

BEAVER DAM
STATION

CHESTERFIELD

NORTH ANNA

SOUTH ANNA

PAMUNKEY

ASHLAND
STATION

TREVILIAN
RAID BEGINS

YELLOW TAVERN

MECHANICSVILLE

RICHMOND

CHICKAHOMINY

ST. MARY'S
CHURCH

SHERIDAN'S   RAIDS

RICHMOND

TREVILIAN

MILES 0   5   10   15   20

JAMES   RIVER

TREVILIAN RAID ENDS

After crossing the Ta River ten miles south of Spotsylvania, Sheridan felt that "our ability to cross the South Anna [was] placed beyond any doubt. However . . . Stuart had discovered what we were about, and he set his cavalry in motion, sending General Fitzhugh Lee to follow and attack my rear on the Childsburg Road, Stuart himself marching . . . toward Beaver Dam Station, near which place his whole command was directed to unite the next day."

Stuart, upon learning of Sheridan's movement, had sent one of Fitz Lee's brigade commanders, W. C. Wickham, in immediate pursuit—a maneuver that Colonel Alfred Gibbs, First New York Dragoons, had good reason to remember. "During the night of the 9th, a squadron were to guard a crossing called Davenport Bridge, where the enemy were busy reconstructing the bridge, and early next morning, after being relieved and on their way to rejoin the column, they were attacked in a defile by . . . Wickham's brigade. Our command suffered severely, losing 2 officers and about 50 men."

On the 10th also, Merritt's men destroyed three trains and ninety wagons and recaptured 300 Federal prisoners at Beaver Dam. They captured nearly all of Lee's medical supplies and a million and a half rations—$7,000,000 worth, one paper said—which the Confederates had moved south for safety; and during that night Sheridan's troops had "thoroughly destroyed" the railroad for several miles in both directions from the station.

As Sheridan pushed on toward Richmond, Stuart "hauled off from my rear, urging his horses to the death in order to get in between Richmond and my column." He just managed to do so, arriving at Yellow Tavern, only six miles from the city, by the next morning, May 11.

Gen. Williams Carter Wickham, C.S.A.

The Sixth Pennsylvania ran into Stuart's men first; Merritt threw forward his reserve brigade in support; Devins' Second Brigade "was thrown in dismounted," Merritt said, "and Custer's 1st moved mounted to the left of the battle line." "The enemy fought with much desperation, employing seriously every available man . . . before the Confederate line broke." A mounted charge, launched by the Fifth Michigan and one of Chapman's regiments, the First Vermont, which was "headed by the intrepid commander of the 1st Brigade, General Custer . . . drove the enemy discomfited from the field. This charge was handsomely executed without loss and resulted in the

137

Col. George H. Chapman and staff, U.S.A.

capture of two guns which had been very annoying."

"Custer's charge," wrote Sheridan, "with Chapman on his flank and the rest of Wilson's division sustaining him, was brilliantly executed. Beginning at a walk, he increased his gait to a trot, and then at full speed rushed at the enemy. At the same moment the dismounted troops . . . moved forward." Stuart's chief of staff told of the next few moments. "On the Telegraph Road . . . about eighty men had collected, and among these the general [Stuart] threw himself, and by his personal example held them steady while the enemy charged entirely past their position. . . . They

were met by a mounted charge of the First Virginia Cavalry and driven back. . . . As they retired, one man who had been dismounted in the charge, and was running out on foot, turned as he passed the general, and discharging his pistol, inflicted the fatal wound."

As he was carried from the field, Stuart raised himself to yell at the retreating Confederates: "Go back! Go back! I had rather die than be whipped." He died in the Richmond home of his brother-in-law after twenty-four hours of dreadful pain. Because of a boyhood promise to his mother, he refused the brandy that might have enabled him to live long enough to see his wife, who was hurrying to

138

his bedside. "All his life was fortunate," John Thomason wrote of him many years after. "It was given to him to toil greatly, to taste no little fame. . . . He died while there was still a thread of hope for victory." Colonel J. S. Green, of Lomax's Brigade, died on the field that day.

"The engagement ended by giving us complete control of the road to Richmond," was Sheridan's comment at the time, but he soon identified its principal accomplishment: Federal cavalry had "inflicted on the Confederate mounted troops the most thorough defeat that had yet befallen them in Virginia." A Southerner remembered, "While Stuart lived, the gray cavalry, man for man and horse for horse, was more effective than anything ever thrown against them."

"Meanwhile," as Sheridan wrote afterwards, "the most intense excitement prevailed in Richmond. The Confederates, supposing that their capital was my objective point, were

Col. John Shac Green, 6th Virginia Cavalry, C.S.A.

Custer's cavalry capture prisoners on the Valley turnpike.

139

Gen. Butler's Headquarters, Bermuda Hundred, James River, Va.

Gen. John B. McIntosh, U.S.A.
(Col. 3rd Pennsylvania Cavalry)

Gen. James B. Gordon, C.S.A.
(*killed at Yellow Tavern, Va., May 11, 1864*)

straining every effort to put it in a state of defense." Braxton Bragg, now military adviser to President Davis, supervised the preparations for defense. But with the Southern cavalry defeated, Sheridan decided that "the main purpose of my instructions had been carried out, and my thoughts then turned to joining General Butler to get supplies." Reconnoitering a route to bypass the city on the north, he discovered that the exterior lines of defense, which were six miles out, were lightly held and that he could move east over an old road between the exterior and interior lines.

He took it before midnight. But his troopers encountered an unexpected weapon in the form of torpedoes that were made of "loaded shells planted on each side of the road, and so connected by wires attached to friction tubes in the shells that when a horse's hoof struck a wire the shell was exploded by the jerk of the improvised lanyard." This hazard Sheridan neutralized by herding his prisoners in front of his men and forcing them to "get down on their knees, feel for the wires in the darkness, and follow them up and unearth the shells."

At daylight, after that tedious night march, Sheridan's advance guard encountered the Confederates at Mechanicsville, waiting for them "in earthworks thrown up across the road." "After forming my brigade about 500 yards from the enemy breastworks," wrote Colonel John McIntosh, "I was ordered to hold. About mid-day the enemy made a determined advance.... We retired." Meanwhile Merritt's entire division was busy repairing Meadow Bridge across the Chickahominy for a return to the north bank. It was slow work, under Confederate artillery and rifle fire and threatened by the advance of a fresh force from Richmond. In this action James Gordon died as his cavalry hacked at Sheridan's rear.

The fight on the south bank was furious. Wilson's men broke once. But as soon as Mer-

Lt. Alexander C. M. Pennington,
2nd U.S. Artillery, U.S.A.

ritt's men had built enough bridgework to permit it, Lieutenant Alex Pennington, of the Second U. S. Artillery, received orders to cross "with 4 of my guns and take position to cover the crossing of the troops. The enemy advanced a strong line of skirmishers almost in my immediate front. I directed my guns upon them and opened." Wilson's men rallied and drove the Confederates back into the Richmond works, where they seemed satisfied that they had completed their job of stopping the raid.

141

Main Street, Richmond. Six miles away Stuart fell, mortally wounded.

The Union soldiers spent what was left of the day resting and observing the city's skyline, grazing their horses, and reading the Richmond journals, which two small boys, "with commendable enterprise," as Sheridan remarked, brought through the lines. When the boys started to return, however, he considered it best to hold them until after the command had crossed the river, since he "thought their mission involved other purposes than the mere sale of newspapers." By the time the main body had finished crossing it was late afternoon, and Merritt's troopers had ranged out to push aside the scattered resistance they encountered. With but slight opposition the whole command reached the Federal lines on the 14th. Sheridan turned over his wounded and prisoners to Butler. "Ample supplies . . . were furnished and the work of refitting for our return . . . was vigorously pushed."

Now heading homeward, Sheridan decided to cross to the north bank of the Pamunkey at White House Landing rather than risk contact with Lee's main army. So he sent down to Fortress Monroe for a pontoon bridge, a five-day supply of rations, and a gunboat to protect his crossing; and when his scouts reported that the enemy cavalry was dropping back to its main army, he rode for White House. He sent Custer's brigade back up to

A Richmond and Fredericksburg Railroad bridge over the North Anna,
set afire by Sheridan's raiders.

The partially ruined covered bridge at Mrs. Nelson's Crossing on the
Pamunkey River.

143

Hanover Station to destroy bridges, and Gregg and Wilson to Cold Harbor to cover his movement with a noisy demonstration, while Merritt took up a blocking position to protect White House. Custer found the crossings of the Richmond and Fredericksburg and the Virginia Central railroads over the North Anna strongly defended; so he did the next best thing, burned two trestle bridges over Hanover Creek. It was just as well, for as Grant's army approached the former bridges three days later, Lee's troops burned them.

On arriving at White House Landing on May 19, Sheridan found that the railroad

Destruction of a Richmond and Fredericksburg Railroad bridge across the North Anna.

144

Sheridan's weary troopers cross the Chesterfield Bridge over the North Anna, en route from Richmond raid. The column suffered 625 casualties in the raid.

bridge which had been reported as destroyed had been only partially so, "the cross-ties and stringers being burned in places only" so "that it was practicable to repair it sufficiently to carry us over," and the pontoon bridge order could be cancelled. "By sending mounted parties through the surrounding country, each man of which would bring in a board or a plank," Merritt soon had sufficient floorboards —a neighboring house melted away in minutes. Stringers were cut from trees; and in fifteen hours the bridge was ready for use. The only accident in the command's crossing was experienced by a mule that slipped off, turned a somersault, and struck a stone abutment. But the animal bobbed up shortly and swam ashore.

On learning from prisoners picked up near Mattapony that Lee had been maneuvered out of his position at Spotsylvania, Sheridan led his weary riders over the North Anna by the bridge at Chesterfield on May 24 and rejoined the Army of the Potomac. Six hundred and twenty-five of his men had been killed or wounded, but Grant was well pleased with his little Irishman: "Sheridan in this memorable raid," he wrote, "passed entirely around Lee's army; encountered his cavalry in four engagements and defeated them in all . . . destroyed and used many supplies and munitions of war . . . [destroyed] miles of railroad and telegraph; and freed us from annoyance by the cavalry of the enemy for more than two weeks."

145

Gen. Alfred T. A. Torbert, U.S.A.

12

Sheridan's Trevilian Raid

U. S. GRANT had the war moving now, and there could be no rest for Sheridan's men. The Army of the Potomac had to have its flanks protected while it crossed the North Anna; confusion must be caused in odd places to keep Lee guessing. "In conjunction with these maneuvers Wilson's division was sent to the right flank of the army, where he made a reconnaissance south of the North Anna as far as Little River. . . . Wilson was to operate from day to day on that flank."

Operate he did, for he joined forces with Federal infantry to destroy methodically miles of Virginia Central trackage. Grant wasted no time now, continuing his new procedure of following each repulse by a movement to Lee's right. He had his eye on the Cold Harbor area —"It was important to us because while there, we covered both the road back to White House

where our supplies came from, and the roads southeast over which we would have to pass to get to the James River below the Richmond defenses."

Sheridan's other two cavalry divisions, Gregg's and Alfred Torbert's, were to run interference. With only intermittent contact with the enemy, "Sheridan was directed to reconnoiter to find out Lee's position. At Hawe's Shop . . . he encountered the Confederate cavalry dismounted and partially entrenched. Gregg attacked . . . but was unable to move the enemy. In the evening Custer came up."

A Richmond paper reported the action: "About 1 o'clock on Saturday, Wickham's brigade, Fitz Lee's division, encountered a large force of the enemy's cavalry near Hawe's shop, about 2 miles this side of Hanover, down the Pamunky. . . . The combat raged with una-

Gen. David Hunter, U.S.A.

bated fury . . . but the effect of the enemy's reenforcements was soon apparent. Our men, being outnumbered, had to withdraw." A Federal participant in the action wrote of it: "It is the first time we have met those Carolinians . . . and I wish to God it might be the last."

The compliment implied was well deserved, earned at the carbine's muzzle. For the Confederate cavalry, like the rest of the Southern army, had suffered terribly from the mere attrition of service during the previous winter. Horses were scarce in the South now and in poor condition. There had been times in the Army of Northern Virginia when a horse's

ration had been no more than three pounds of corn a day, and the men had fared no better; while on the Federal side a magnificent remount service kept its riders well mounted, food was plentiful, and the troopers had begun to be armed with repeating carbines. "You all must sit up all night loadin' them new guns of yours," was the comment of a Confederate prisoner.

Grant, well aware of the soundness of one Southerner's estimate of the situation, that "the railroad is our backbone," determined to keep the strain on that backbone. He summoned Sheridan again and ordered: "With two

148

divisions . . . you will move on the morning of the 7th [of June] to Charlottesville and destroy the railroad bridge . . . then thoroughly destroy the railroad . . . to Gordonsville and toward Hanover Junction." And since Federal General David Hunter's command had been ordered from the Shenandoah toward Charlottesville, Sheridan understood that Grant "expected me to unite with [Hunter] there, and . . . after destroying the James River Canal and the Virginia Central road . . . join the Army of the Potomac."

Leaving Wilson with the Army of the Potomac, Sheridan headed northwest with Gregg's and Torbert's divisions and bivouacked on the night of June 10th four miles from Trevilian

Station. But Wade Hampton had been "up and doing." He started one day behind Sheridan, but he had a shorter distance to go and, making all speed, succeeded in placing his command between Sheridan and the enemy's objective. By the night of the 10th he had reached Green Spring Valley, three miles from Trevilian, and went into camp there. At nearly the same time Fitzhugh Lee's division reached Louisa Court House, about five miles from Trevilian, and it was now pretty well known among those veterans that Hampton was seeking Sheridan.

Torbert's column set out about five o'clock next morning and encountered the enemy almost immediately after leaving camp. As

Cavalry Scouting

Pvt. David A. Meade, 3rd Virginia Cavalry, C.S.A.

the carbines crackled in front, Custer's brigade, which had been sent by a side road to burn the station, struck the Confederate rear and captured the wagons and caissons parked there. Nothing daunted, Hampton turned Rosser's brigade around to face Custer and went on fighting. "Our losses were severe," said a Federal participant of the fighting that day. "Colonel Sackett, Ninth New York, was mortally wounded while gallantly leading his regiment into action, and several other officers and many brave men fell before the station was carried."

"During the afternoon," when the fight had rolled past the station, "the railroad . . . was

Federal tents are pitched at White House, burned earlier in the war.

150

thoroughly torn up." The two Confederate divisions, which fought separately during that day, were united by noon of the day following at Mallory's Crossroads. Torbert's dismounted troopers attacked the dismounted Confederates. But Hampton had Fitzhugh Lee take L. L. Lomax's brigade "across to the Gordonsville road so as to strike the enemy on his right flank," and "the enemy fell back in confusion." A Federal prisoner's diary gave a concise chronology of the action: "Saturday, June 11. Fight at Trevilian Station. Captured and killed 600 rebs. Sunday, June 12th, Fought on same ground. Got whipped like the devil. Lost more men than the rebs did the day previous. Monday, June 13th, Retreat back towards Fredericksburg."

Learning from his prisoners that "General Hunter, instead of coming toward Charlottesville . . . was in the neighborhood of Lexington . . . marching away from instead of towards

Lt. Col. William Sackett, 9th New York Cavalry, U.S.A.
(*killed June 11, 1864*)

The gunboat *Commodore Perry* and a monitor on the James.

Pontoon bridge above Jones's Landing on the James River.

me," Sheridan wisely backtracked across the North Anna, paused a little to graze his horses, which had not eaten for two days, and headed for Spotsylvania. The column moved slowly because of walking prisoners and wounded men; and, Sheridan recorded: "Where all the colored people came from and what started them was inexplicable, but they began joining us just before we reached Trevilian. . . . to a man they followed the Yankees in full faith." An occasional Federal rider sympathized with some prisoner coughing in the heat of the dusty road and exchanged places with him. They marched over the Spotsylvania battlefield on June 15. "The marks of the recent conflicts were visible on every hand, and in the neighboring houses were found many wounded. . . . Such as were able to travel were brought away."

Hampton had seen the pontoon bridge that Sheridan had with him, and since it gave the Federals the ability to cross the North Anna or the Pamunkey at any point, he moved by a parallel route as they marched slowly southward. "Embarrassed as I was with . . . wounded . . . prisoners, and about 2,000 wagons," Sheridan hesitated to venture between the Mattaponi and the Pamunkey rivers. He finally crossed the former and on June 21 reached White House Landing.

152

Capt. Alanson M. Randol, 2nd New York Cavalry, U.S.A.

ol. George S. Nichols, 9th New York Cavalry, U.S.A.

Grant by this time had shifted his base to the James. Sheridan received orders to break up the base at White House Landing and, "bringing its garrison and an immense wagon-train with him," to march to Charles City Court House and thence to the pontoon bridge over the James at Deep Bottom. With the problem of escorting a slow and unwieldy train of 900 wagons across what amounted to the front of the enemy army, Sheridan sent Torbert's division to secure the Chickahominy Bridge and Gregg's to guard the exposed right flank of his long column.

It was well that he took these precautions. The Confederate cavalry under J. R. Chambliss struck at Torbert on the 23rd but could not prevent the Federals' crossing the Chickahominy. It was necessary, however, to park the long wagon train near Wilcox's Landing while Gregg's men fought it out with Hampton's at St. Mary's Church. Hampton attacked

153

Col. George H. Covode, 4th Pennsylvania Cavalry, U.S.A.
(*killed at St. Mary's Church, Va., June 24, 1864*)

fiercely, using Fitzhugh Lee against the Federal front and two brigades in a flanking movement.

"Between 3 and 4 p.m.," Gregg recorded, "the enemy made an attack in great force . . . on the right of our line. . . . The strife was in earnest now; there were no disengaged men on our side. Randol's and Dennison's batteries (H and I) pitched load after load of cannister into the staggering lines of the enemy." But the gray horsemen fought furiously, and Hampton recorded with satisfaction: "The enemy were completely routed . . . the pursuit lasting

Members of the Sussex Light Dragoons, Troop H, 13th Virginia Cavalry, which fought against Sheridan in the Trevilian raid.

A Union skirmish line moves forward.

until 10 o'clock at night. We captured 157 prisoners, including 1 colonel and 12 commissioned officers."

"Gregg's losses were heavy," a Federal report admitted, "and he was forced to abandon his dead and most seriously wounded." The dead included Lieutenant Colonel George H. Covode. But although the price was high, Gregg's action made it possible for the wagon train to edge past before "he retired . . . in some confusion, it is true, but stubbornly resisting"; and not one wagon was lost. With the column halted at Charles City Court House, however, Sheridan observed, "Gregg's fight fully convinced me that we could not get the trains up to the pontoon bridge." Meade had come to the same conclusion and had ordered up ferry boats to move Sheridan across the James, for he was growing anxious about Wilson, who had been sent to break up the railroads to the south and west of Petersburg and Richmond. With gunboats covering the crossing, it was completed by June 29.

Sheridan had been busy in his new job; no longer was there a sting in that jibing query, "Whoever saw a dead cavalryman?" His musters showed 5000 casualties, and a loss of 2000 men taken prisoners. "In all the operations," he stated, "the percentage of cavalry casualties was as great as that of the infantry."

Gen. James H. Wilson, U.S.A.

Wilson and Kautz
on Lee's Back

Union Bugler

WITH SHERIDAN'S command incapacitated for the time being by their recent exertions, the Confederate cavalry could concentrate on a second danger point, which was one of the greatest importance. For the commander of Sheridan's Third Division, young Brigadier General James Harrison Wilson, of Shawneetown, Illinois—"a slight person of a light complexion and with a rather pinched face"—was doing a methodical job of destruction on the vital railroads south of Petersburg.

The twenty-seven-year-old Wilson had been in the engineers until he was placed in charge of the Federal Cavalry Bureau in February 1864. Only on the 4th of May had he received the command of one of Sheridan's cavalry divisions. He had much to learn, as his service in the wilderness had demonstrated. But he learned quickly and was capable and daring. His instructions now were to strike the railroad as close as practicable to Petersburg and destroy it in the direction of Burkeville and the Roanoke River. The High Bridge on the South Side Railroad and the Roanoke Bridge on the Danville line were especially to be aimed at.

His return route was left to his discretion. He might, if he found it best to do so, cross into North Carolina and move to the coast, or he might join General Sherman in North Georgia. Or he could return to the Army of the Potomac by any route that might prove to be most practicable. Considering the last course would turn out to be the best, he asked that Sheridan should keep Hampton occupied, and that the Federal infantry do the like

157

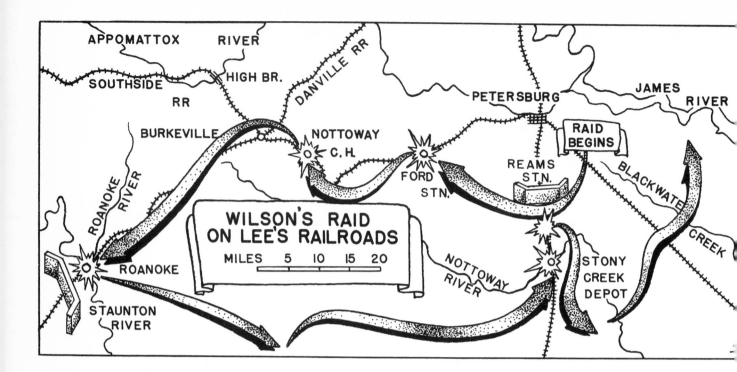

WILSON'S RAID ON LEE'S RAILROADS

MILES 5 10 15 20

Gen. Robert F. Hoke, C.S.A.

with their Confederate counterparts. Meade explained that his plan provided for that: he would have infantry astride the Weldon Railroad the next day, and the South Side Railroad the day after.

Before he left, Wilson had been reinforced by Brigadier General A. V. Kautz with four cavalry regiments from Butler's Army of the James. Kautz, a West Pointer, from Georgetown, Ohio, had cut the railroad below Petersburg two months before this in order to delay Beauregard's reinforcement of Lee's army. On June 22, 1864, his troops spearheading the expedition, Kautz rode from his Blackwater Creek base at two in the morning. Encountering little opposition in his front and helped by Wilson's rear-guard fighting, he pushed on rapidly to Ford's Station. There he captured two railroad trains and their locomotives, burned the depot, water-tanks, and woodpiles, and worked until late at night tearing up the railroad track and burning the ties.

158

During that afternoon General Robert E. Lee notified Richmond: "From all I can learn the enemy's cavalry are moving through Dinwiddie inquiring the road to Burkeville and the High Bridge on the South Side Railroad." The next morning he learned of Federal infantry astride the Weldon line. Soon after, he could report, "before they had done much damage" they "were driven back by General Mahone," who took "about 600 prisoners." Thus early was Wilson's shortest line of retirement imperiled.

During the second day of the raid Kautz rode hard for Burkeville, eighty miles to the west of Petersburg, while Wilson pushed the rest of his 5000-man force after him. Delayed by following a wrong road, Wilson was overtaken by "Rooney" Lee's cavalry at Nottoway Court House. "From 1 p.m. until 9 the contest was continued with considerable intensity,"

Gen. William Mahone, C.S.A.

At Ford's Station, Kautz burned the depot, water tanks, and woodpiles and captured two locomotives.

Wilson reported, "the enemy making several determined efforts to drive us from the railroad. This was one of the most determined cavalry engagements in which this division has participated. . . . Our loss was about 75." He might have added that this unexpected opposition struck the High Bridge off his target list.

Deeply concerned about Kautz, Wilson threw forward a squadron under Captain W. W. Whittaker. But Kautz was having a high time. In Burkeville by the middle of that afternoon, Kautz "proceeded at once to the destruction of the roads leading toward Richmond and toward Lynchburg . . . several miles destroyed in every direction." He was unper-

turbed by Whittaker's news of the fighting in his rear and led his men down the Danville Railroad before dawn of the next day (June 24), detaching parties at intervals to destroy the track. When Wilson joined him that evening, "the whole command continued work till all the track in the vicinity of its camps had been completely destroyed." On the following day Wilson saw to it that "every depot, turn-table, water-tank, and trestle-work between the Sixteen-Mile Turnout on the South Side Railroad and the Roanoke Bridge on the Danville road was destroyed."

At dusk the next day the raiders descended on Roanoke Station, where Kautz tried to capture the Staunton River Bridge. But it was defended with determination "by six guns in position in works on the south side of the river and four lines of rifle trench between them and the river bank, manned by the militia of eight counties." Colonel Robert M. West took a squadron of his Fifth Pennsylvania, "skirmishing to within 200 yards of the main bridge, where we came to a small bridge. . . . Under cover of this bridge I formed an assaulting party and directed it up the embankment, in the hope that by a quick move we might obtain possession of the main bridge sufficiently long to fire it. The men tried repeatedly to gain a foothold [but] the height of the railroad embankment enabled the enemy . . . to sweep the sides and tracks with a terrible fire."

Wilson now very nearly got himself trapped; "Rooney" Lee's horsemen struck his rear with all the determination of their previous attacks. His position "was rather dangerous," he admitted, "and in order to extricate the command it became necessary to move it by night . . . along the foot of the bluffs," leaving thirty of his men dead behind him. Anxious to avoid contact with the enemy, he pushed eastward, allowing his weary horses and men only a halt for coffee at daybreak. But at dark that day Hampton's horsemen again fell upon him at Stony Brook Depot. After a fight that lasted until ten o'clock they forced him to seek another route.

He had reason to expect that Ream's Station, a few miles farther north, would be held by Union forces, and he pushed Kautz toward that point. But instead of the infantry of the Army of the Potomac, Kautz found there a

Gen. August V. Kautz and Gen. Godfrey Weitzel, U.S.A.

161

The weariness of the troopers led by Kautz, returning from their raid on the railroads, is caught in this drawing.

division of rebel infantry strongly posted. "He ... was compelled to withdraw ... completely routed," according to "Rooney" Lee. Wilson, badly shaken and "fearing the loss of my entire command without the utmost promptitude and rapidity of movement, ordered the issue of all the ammunition the troops could carry, and immediate destruction of the wagons and caissons." But Southern infantry scattered his rear-guard and captured them; and on one of them, to the disgrace of the Northern troopers, was found the silver communion service belonging to St. John's Church in Lunenburg County, according to one incensed Southerner.

Colonel West, who succeeded in rallying a thousand of the disorganized troopers, was compelled to lead them through the woods by compass, with "some inconvenience ... from small parties of the enemy who were concealed." Wilson managed to hold most of his immediate command together. He swung south of the Nottoway, then east and north to the Blackwater, only "to find the bridge gone and the stream utterly unfordable. I immediately began the repair and ... soon had it fit for crossing by file, but the materials having been partly burned, gave way." Working in darkness, the raiders again repaired the bridge only

to see it slide into the water after a few more men had crossed. New string-pieces were cut from the woods, and by three in the morning it was again "covered with rails" and ready for use. The whole command was over by 6:15 a.m.

It was Saturday, July 2, when the command reached safety at Light House Point on the James. The previous ten days had been grueling: four major fights and 335 miles of marching, without one adequate rest period. But Wilson estimated that he had destroyed sixty miles of track, and that it would be more than two months before supply trains rolled into Richmond and Petersburg from the south and west. For this, to be sure, the enemy had exacted a bloody price—1500 Federal officers and soldiers killed, wounded, and missing.

Wilson's raiders tear a railroad track apart.

163

The High Bridge of the South Side Railroad, spanning the Appomattox
River, was a target for one of Sheridan's raiding cavalry divisions led by
General Wilson.

The 5th U.S. Cavalry in camp.

When, some years later, Grant considered the effects of the raids of the Union cavalry, his opinion was that they "contributed very little to the grand result." But it has always been difficult for an infantryman to appreciate the exploits of the cavalry. It is true that the lines damaged by Wilson were in operation, after a fashion, sixty days later. But the destroyed locomotives and rolling stock were irreplaceable in the South, and the stock of rails was running low. There had never been enough of them since the war began. When the president of the Southern railroads met in Richmond the previous winter, they had "ascertained," according to a Richmond War Department clerk, "that to keep the tracks in order for military purposes 49,500 tons of rails must be manufactured per annum, and that the Tredegar Works here [at Richmond], and the works at Atlanta cannot produce more than 20,000 tons per annum, even if engaged exclusively in that work."

General Jubal Early, C.S.A.

14

Sheridan Cleans the Shenandoah

THIS SAME JUNE 1864 saw the beginning of another famous Confederate raid—one which, although it was accomplished for the most part by infantry, was notable for a swiftness and audacity that would have done credit to mounted troops. To relieve the steadily increasing pressure on his lines around Richmond, Lee adopted the strategy with which Stonewall Jackson had been so successful two years before in the Shenandoah Valley. Jackson was dead, but dependable "Old Jubilee" [J. A.] Early could be relied upon to act with all Jackson's vigor and nerve, and western Virginia was his home country.

By the middle of June Early had sent the Federal force under General David Hunter flying into the mountains of West Virginia.

He swept down the Shenandoah Valley, chased General Franz Sigel's troops out of Martinsburg early in July, and fed with captured supplies his hungry soldiers, who in the past two weeks had fought and marched 400 miles with a spirit and celerity that recalled the days of Jackson's "foot cavalry." Fording the Potomac, he turned southeastward—toward Washington —driving Federal detachments before him and giving Hagerstown and Frederick a dose of war's unpleasantness by putting them to ransom on threat of destruction.

On the afternoon of the 11th of July he was at the end of Seventh Street, on the very edge of Washington. He could see the dome of the capitol; and President Lincoln, watching his advance from the parapet of Fort Stevens,

The Chambersburg town fathers did not take a Confederate demand for ransom seriously. As a result Col. Gilmor's Maryland Cavalry, at McCausland's order, burned much of the Pennsylvania town.

came under the fire of his skirmishers. But there were too many Federal troops in Washington for him to attack the city. At all events his threat had compelled Grant to send up two divisions from the James to insure its defense. So Early marched homeward by way of Leesburg, driving large herds of cattle before him, having burned only a single house —that of Postmaster General Montgomery Blair, who had been Dred Scott's legal counsel.

When he got back to the Shenandoah, however, and had chased George Crook's Federals out of Martinsburg, he learned that Hunter had returned to the Valley and done great damage there. "A number of towns in the South, as well as private houses, had been burned," and Early "came to the conclusion that it was time to open the eyes of the people of the North to this enormity, by an example in the way of retaliation."

He selected Chambersburg, Pennsylvania, as the target, and ordered Brigadier General John McCausland "to proceed with his brigade and that of Johnson and a battery of artillery to that place, and demand of the municipal authorities the sum of $100,000 in gold or $500,000 in U. S. currency, as compensation for the destruction of the houses named and their contents; and in default of payment, to lay the town in ashes."

McCausland's command—2600 men and six cannon—materialized from the fairground overlooking Chambersburg in the pre-dawn darkness of July 30. He drew a ring of men around the place; and the bursting of two shells from his howitzers in the middle of the sleeping community announced the arrival of a detachment under Brigadier General Bradley Johnson. As a surprised Federal army clerk recorded it: "They entered then by almost every alley and by-street by small squads prior to the advance of the main body, which came up directly."

McCausland grabbed this clerk and told him, "It would be well . . . to get the municipal authorities together," and that it must be done within three hours or the town would be destroyed. Upon meeting one of the town coun-

Brig. Gen. John McCausland, C.S.A.

cil, the clerk "informed him of the facts," only to be told that "the citizens would not pay five cents." They apparently considered the threat a bluff. "The policy of our army on former occasions," as Early put it, "had been so lenient that they did not suppose the threat was in earnest this time, and they hoped for speedy relief."

McCausland wasted no time after the clerk brought the message back to the porch of the Franklin Hotel; and at the instruction, "The town must be burnt," Major Harry Gilmor's Maryland cavalry fell to work. A Union man watched "details made up and placed under charge of officers and fires kindled . . . almost simultaneously in fifty different places. . . . Some of the officers and men refused, or were persuaded not to carry out their barbarous orders, and assisted people in fleeing from the

169

Not much of the northwest corner of Chambersburg's public square was left when the Confederate raiders had gone.

Gen. Bradley Johnson, c.s.a.

flames. . . . In a few moments the commissary store-house was in flames, during which time McCausland and Gilmor were riding through town notifying the citizens. . . . The right and left sides of the main street [soon became] one mass of flames."

As McCausland anticipated, there was more than a little consternation among the highest Federal authorities. Halleck telegraphed Department Commander D. N. Couch: "Can you give any definite information of the enemy's force which entered Chambersburg? Was it a cavalry raid or the main army?" And Secretary of War Stanton echoed with a caustic: "The Department would be glad to have some information from you . . . regarding the enemy and . . . steps taken toward defense." Couch

170

Generals of the Union Cavalry Corps: from left to right, Merritt, Gregg, Sheridan, Davies, Wilson, and Torbert.

replied that the Governor of Pennsylvania had "made an appeal to the people" but "his course of action had not been decided upon. . . . I shall order up the provost and hospital guards at Philadelphia."

By this time the Confederates had left. "As soon as the city was fairly burning," Johnson recorded, "we moved on McConnellsburg"; they bivouacked late in the afternoon. While they ate a late Sunday lunch at Hancock, McCausland demanded a $30,000 ransom from the town. But pursuit was now pressing too close to allow either the collection of the money or the burning of the town. A week later, when he had his force resting in camp at Moorefield in West Virginia, W. W. Averell's cavalry routed both brigades.

On August 11, 1864, Theodore Lyman noted: "Sheridan has been appointed to command all the upper Potomac forces, which is saying that he is to command all the troops to drive Early out of the Shenandoah Valley. He is a major general, and is an energetic and brave officer.

Gen. William Averell, U.S.A.

This command, however, is a very large one, larger than he ever before had. I have little doubt that, for field service, he is superior to any officer there. Things are cooking. . . ." The result was Early backing cautiously before Sheridan to Strasburg.

"Well, we tramped down the Shenandoah Valley, and we tramped back again," wrote a Union captain to his wife. "If ever I volunteer again I shall specify that I am not to make war in it." He guessed that the endless marching was because "General Sheridan is cautious about fighting. . . . With so many elections at hand . . . it would not do to have this army beaten." That was, in fact, exactly the way Sheridan looked at it: "The defeat of my army might be followed by the overthrow of the party in power." And that could mean peace

171

Hon. Andrew G. Curtin, Governor of Pennsylvania.

Union cavalry chase Early's men through Strasburg. After the victories
at Opequon and Strasburg, Sheridan was master of the Valley.

without victory, which was what the Southerners had long been hoping for.

"It seemed to us," wrote one of the Gray cavalrymen, "that for every [Northern soldier] killed or captured half a dozen would rise up in their places. When we lost a man he was dead for certain. . . . None was to be had to stand in his place." But there was hope for the South in the "deadly weary feeling creeping over the North about the war. People were becoming shy of the attrition process." If the Democrats should win the election up there this fall . . .

Grant, however, decided to get on with the war, election or no election, and ordered Sheridan to "attack Early, drive him out of the Valley, and destroy that source of supplies for Lee's army." "We commenced moving north," wrote William DeForest, of Sheridan's army, "the Eighth Corps leading. . . . Behind came the cavalry, in a broad line from mountain to mountain, burning the mills and barns and driving off the cattle and sheep. Between Mount Crawford and Woodstock over seventy mills and two thousand barns, crammed with flour, wheat, corn and hay, were destroyed.

The inhabitants were left so stripped of food that I cannot imagine how they escaped starvation."

A Federal order to Virginia citizens read: "You are hereby notified that for every train fired upon, or soldier of the Union wounded or assassinated by bushwhackers in any neighborhood within the reach of my cavalry, the houses and other property of every secession sympathizer residing within a circuit of five miles from the place of outrage shall be destroyed by fire, and that for all public property jayhawked or destroyed by these marauders, an assessment of five times the value of such property will be made upon the secession sympathizers residing within a circuit of ten miles around the point at which the offense was committed. The payment of

Brig. Gen. John D. Imboden, C.S.A.

Confederate raiders wrap the rails of the Orange and Alexandria Railroad, near Bristoe Station, Va., in fire.

173

Federal cavalry scout in the Blue Ridge.

this assessment will be enforced by troops of the department, who will seize and hold in close custody the persons assessed until such payment shall have been made."

John Mosby hurled fierce attacks on Sheridan's forces. At Berryville he swept down with 200 rangers upon Sheridan's wagons and completely routed the guard, killing or wounding several and taking more than 200 prisoners, including three lieutenants. He destroyed 75 loaded wagons and captured upwards of 200 beef cattle and between 500 and 600 horses and

174

mules, with a loss of but two killed and three wounded of his own men. Sheridan's board of inquiry spent two months trying to find a scapegoat for this affair. The audacious partisan leader's September report showed that in recent weeks he had paid for 1200 Federals killed, wounded, and captured, 1600 horses, and 230 beef cattle with a casualty list of no more than twenty of his rangers.

The galled Sheridan had to admit that there had been "so much detached service to protect trains, and to secure Maryland and Pennsylvania from raids, that my excess in numbers was almost cancelled." He aimed for the spot where Mosby and his like were most vulnerable, the territory that gave him refuge and supplies. "In retaliation for the assistance and sympathy given" the rangers, he sent Merritt into Loudoun Valley with two cavalry brigades under orders to "consume and destroy all forage and subsistance, burn all barns and mills and their contents, and drive off all stock," with the specification that "this order must be literally executed." That night, a ranger recalled grimly, "blazing fires were visible in all directions. . . . I was carried back to Attila, with his fierce barbarians."

In the line of regular warfare Sheridan defeated Early on September 22 at Fisher's Hill. But he was so disappointed in the handling of his mounted troops that day that, as he reported to Grant: "I have relieved Averell from his command. Instead of following the enemy when he was broken at Fisher's Hill . . . he went into camp and let me pursue the enemy for a distance of 15 miles with infantry during the night." As one of Sheridan's foot soldiers put it: "The cavalry were less fervent, or perhaps less fortunate, in carrying out orders. Torbert, who had been sent to the Luray Valley to intercept Early's flight, recoiled from a strong position at Milford held

The 5th Michigan Cavalry, guidons flying, charge at Opequon.

Gen. Lunsford L. Lomax, c.s.a.

Gen. George Custer, u.s.a.

176

Custer's Division, devastating the Shenandoah Valley, leaves the barns
near Mount Jackson smoking.

by Lomax's mounted riflemen." A New York
cavalryman admitted: "At long range we are
rather afraid of them. They carry Enfields,
which shoot farther than our carbines."

Among a number of brilliant actions, those
of Sheridan's cavalry at Winchester and Cedar
Creek gained a special fame. While Sheridan
was on his return from a brief absence in
Washington, his forces came near being routed
at Cedar Creek on October 19. At Winchester,
twenty miles away, he heard the noise of
battle and made for it at his horse's best
speed. He arrived on the field "at a tearing
trot, swinging his hat and shouting . . . 'about
face, boys! We are going back to our camps.
We are going to lick them out of their boots.'"
By afternoon his men were advancing to yet
another victory. As one of them grumbled,

Col. Alfred N. Duffie, 1st Rhode Island and 2nd New York Cavalry, U.S.A.

"We may as well whip them tonight; if we don't, we shall have to do it tomorrow. Sheridan will get it out of us sometime."

By early November Mosby had plucked another general from under Federal noses. Riding with 300 rangers against Sheridan's rear, he spotted a lightly escorted spring wagon some distance ahead of a Union supply column near Bunker Hill; and, in answer to his demand for the name of the senior officer riding in it

he received the nervous reply, "General Duffie." Duffie, a cavalry division commander, who had been praised for brilliant action at Kelly's Ford, had good reason for nervousness at being captured by the partisan chief. He was believed to have ordered his men to shoot all prisoners taken from Mosby's command. The example had been set by Custer, who had recently shot three rangers and hanged three more at Front Royal, with the notice "Such is the fate of all

Mosby's men" fastened to their swinging bodies. But Duffie, much to his relief, learned that Mosby was saving his revenge for Custer and that he was to be made a prisoner of war like the other 700 Federals Mosby had captured since the hanging. Within the next week, however, Mosby's men had whipped the horses out from under three of Custer's troopers, hanging them in reprisal for their commander's action. Two more were shot, and two others broke away.

But all the audacity, courage, and skill in the world cannot succeed against starvation. The Confederate forces in the Valley melted away that winter. For, as Sheridan put it, "a crow would have had to carry its rations if it had flown across the valley." The Shenandoah campaign was over.

Sheridan's Ride as an artist visualized it.

The 6th U.S. Cavalry, sketched in camp at Snicker's Gap, Va., November 29, 1864, were employed in raiding Loudoun County, Va., and laying waste "Mosby's Confederacy."

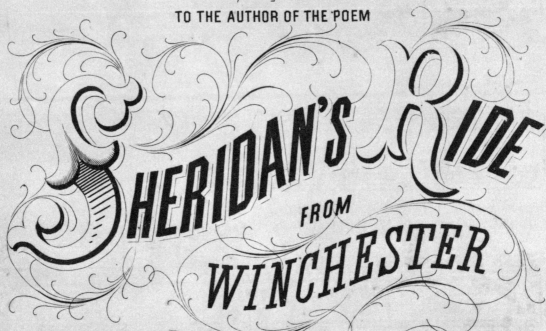

Respectfully Dedicated
TO THE AUTHOR OF THE POEM

Sheridan's Ride

FROM

WINCHESTER

SONG AND CHORUS

written by

T. BUCHANAN READ

composed by

DAVID A. WARDEN.

L. E. Swain.

3½

PHILADELPHIA

Published by Chas. W. A. Trumpler 7th & Chestnut St.

| Boston | Cin. | Chicago | Boston |
| D. Ditson & Co. | J. Church Jr. | Lyon & Healy. | J. C. Haynes & Co. |

Ent. according to Act of Congress A.D.1865 by D. A. Warden in the Clerks Office of the Dist. Court for En. Dist. of Pa.

Sheridan's Ride inspired songwriters.

Sheridan's Ride

WRITTEN BY T. BUCHANAN READ.   COMPOSED BY DAVID A. WARDEN.

Sheridan's Ride from Winchester.

182

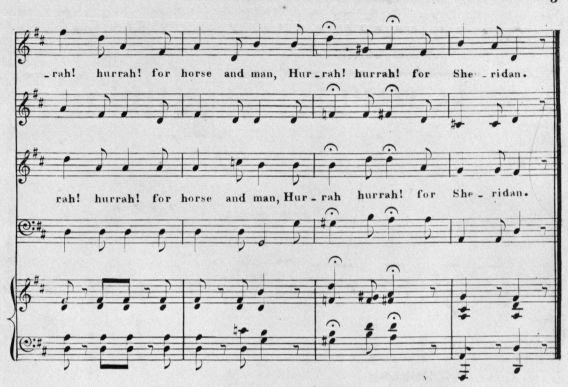

_rah! hurrah! for horse and man, Hur_rah! hurrah! for She_ridan.

rah! hurrah! for horse and man, Hur_rah hurrah! for She_ridan.

3

But there is a road from Winchester town,
A good, broad highway, leading down;
And there thro' the flash of the morning light,
A steed as black as the steeds of night
Was seen to pass as with eagle flight —
As if he knew the terrible need
He stretched away with his utmost speed;
Hill rose and fell— but his heart was gay,
With Sheridan fifteen miles away.

4

Still sprung from those swift hoofs, thundering South,
The dust, like the smoke from the cannon's mouth,
Or the trail of a comet sweeping faster and faster,
Foreboding to traitors the doom of disaster;
The heart of the steed and the heart of the master
Where beating like prisoners assaulting their walls,
Impatient to be where the battle field calls;
Every nerve of the charger was strained to full play,
With Sheridan only ten miles away.

5

Under his spurning feet the road
Like an arrowy alpine river flowed,
And the landscape sped away behind
Like an ocean flying before the wind;
And the steed, like a bark fed with furnace ire,
Swept on, with his wild eyes full of fire,
But, lo! he is nearing his heart's desire—
He is snuffing the smoke of the roaring fray,
With Sheridan only five miles away.

Sheridan's Ride from Winchester.

Gen. Wade Hampton, C.S.A.

15

Spur worn by Gen. Edward Moody McCook, U.S.A.

Hampton's Beefsteaks

FROM BEHIND the battered Richmond-Petersburg lines the Confederate cavalry was to flare out briefly once more in a reminder of its former glory. Lee's senior cavalryman, Wade Hampton, had finally taken over the dead Stuart's job of cavalry chief, eliminating the confusion that had resulted from directing three cavalry divisions from army headquarters. The assignment had been postponed, it seemed, from spite. In March, according to Hampton's confidence to Mary Chesnut, "Stuart had taken one of Hampton's brigades and given it to Fitzhugh Lee. General Hampton complained of this to General Lee, who told him curtly: 'I would not care if you went back to South Carolina with your whole division.'" It was an ill-considered retort. The mortified Hampton had no peer among Lee's kin.

A good judge of such matters has said: "A cavalry leader must be able both to think and to act with the rapidity of a flash of lightning, and that Hampton did." The forty-six-year-old South Carolinian, whose great-grandfather had been killed in an Indian massacre, had come by his military ability naturally. His grandfather had ridden with Washington and served in the War of 1812, when Wade's father had fought under Andrew Jackson. Believed to be the South's wealthiest planter, Wade had recruited the Hampton Legion and received his first wound while leading it at First Manassas. Joining Stuart, he had campaigned with him through Yellow Tavern.

Grant's supply base at City Point, Va., was a target for Wade Hampton and his squadrons.

The idea of raiding the supply area of the Federal army in the early fall of 1864 was based on the report of a scout, Sergeant George Shadburne, which was dated September 5. "I have just returned from City Point," Shadburne stated. "At Coggins Point are 3,000 beeves, attended by 120 men and thirty citizens without arms. At Sycamore Church is one regiment of cavalry (First District of Columbia). This is the nearest point of the picket line to Coggins Point."

Hampton at once saw the opportunity to raise the meat ration of Lee's lean-ribbed soldiers. He "selected Sycamore Church . . . as the point to attack, as being the most central, the nearest to the cattle, and the one where the largest force of the enemy was camped. By dispersing them here I made it impossible for them to concentrate . . . in time to interfere."

On September 14, he eased his squadrons down the west bank of Rowanty Creek, around the left flank of the Union lines before Petersburg, and next morning led them to a bridge over the Blackwater which the Federals had burned and therefore deleted from their list of picket stations. That afternoon, as his troopers rested and fed, an engineer party threw up a bridge, and the command crossed at midnight.

"Rooney" Lee "was directed to move . . . to the stage road at which point he would encounter the first pickets. . . . These he was to drive in . . . then occupy the roads leading from the direction of the enemy at Sycamore Church. General . . . Dearing was . . . to pro-

ceed to Cook's Mill," where he was to hold until the center column's attack on the cattle guards, then "dash across to the Minger's Ferry road . . . guarding against an attack from Fort Powhatan."

The raiders moved on schedule, without alerting the enemy, and at 5 a.m., Rosser's column attacked. Jumping off at the signal of Rosser's guns, Lee and Dearing "established themselves rapidly and firmly at the points they were ordered to secure." Lee's horsemen burst out of the night around the First District of Columbia cavalry camps in Kautz's

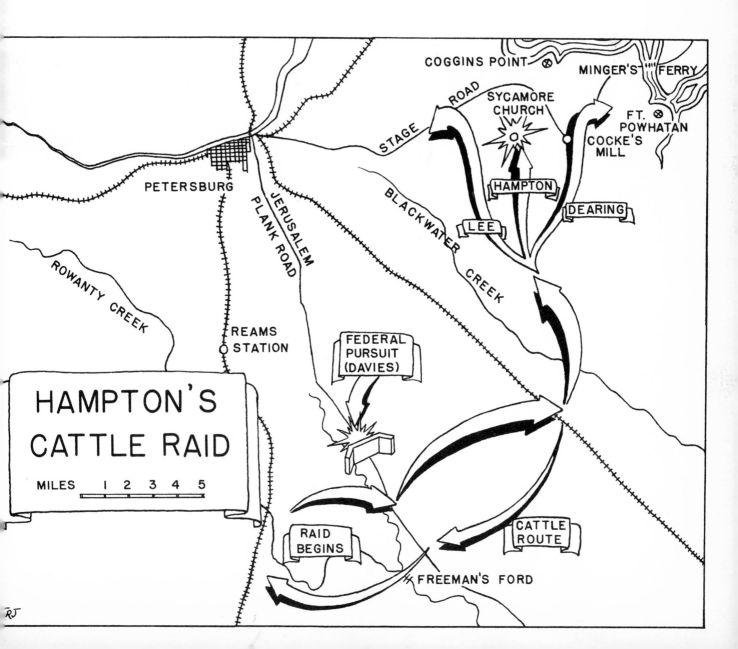

HAMPTON'S CATTLE RAID

MILES   1 2 3 4 5

Hampton's cavalry capture the cattle corral at Coggin's Point from the
13th Pennsylvania.

picket line. Before the enemy troopers could jump to the defense, "the greater portion of the officers of the regiment were captured, together with the company papers," Kautz grumbled, "which will render the transfer of the officers and men of this regiment . . . somewhat troublesome." A later muster showed 212 missing.

With both flanks protected from interference, Hampton's "rustlers" captured the cattle corral from the Thirteenth Pennsylvania. Here, too, the move was so quick that "no effort was made by the cattle guard to let the cattle out or to stampede them," Kautz stated. Wasting little time, Hampton "withdrew everything before 8 a.m. The different columns were

Gen. Henry E. Davies, Jr., U.S.A.

united before reaching the Blackwater, and all dispositions made to protect our captured property."

Brigadier General H. E. Davies, Jr., sent Kautz in pursuit via Sycamore Church and himself took a division to intercept the raiders on the Jerusalem Plank Road. But Hampton had foreseen this movement, and screened the retreat of the column with the cattle by throwing across the Plank Road forces that

constructed a position that Davies found too strong to be taken. To Hampton's delight, however, he kept on trying until eight o'clock that night, when the cattle column was safely past.

With little effort Lee's troopers held Kautz off the column's rear, and Kautz's only accomplishment was the recovery of "some fifty head of cattle left on the road." "The Federal herders of the cattle proved very useful," one

Gen. Edward W. Whittaker, U.S.A.

191

Officers of the 1st Massachusetts Cavalry, U.S.A., Petersburg, Va., August 1864.
(Seated in the rocking chair is Capt. Charles Francis Adams, Jr.)

rustler wrote, "and served their new masters as well and apparently as readily as if these had been their original employers. When the oxen would become troublesome, showing an inclination to stray into the fields and make delay, the herders, cracking their long lashes, sounding like pistol-shots, would quickly bring them back, though it must be confessed a trooper always rode alongside . . . to insure loyalty."

Gen. U. S. Grant, U.S.A. with his favorite charger "Cincinnati."

192

Longhorns: Beef for the Army of the Potomac.

To expedite the march the huge herd had been formed into "detachments with intervals between each," and "Hampton's steaks" were soon in the Confederate commissary. Meade notified Grant: "I deem it proper to call to your attention the small force of cavalry under my command. . . . In the presence of the enemy's superior forces this arm of the service is unable to accomplish anything." And the next day a Federal Fifth Corps order read: "All officers . . . having horses, not entitled to them by regulations, will report the same to this headquarters by the 20th."

193

Sgt. Joshua P. Graffam, 1st District of Columbia Cavalry, U.S.A.

Gen. Samuel D. Sturgis, U.S.A.

Confederate lance
or guidon pennant.

16

"That Devil Forrest"

EANWHILE, down in Georgia and out in Tennessee the Confederate cavalry had been far from idle that summer and fall of 1864. General Joseph Johnston, Bragg's successor, had found in it an excellent means of delaying Sherman's advance on Atlanta, and it had headed the Confederate General J. B. Hood's advance on Nashville. Reports of Confederate cavalry strength in Mississippi and eastern Louisiana, Johnston recorded, "gave me reason to hope that an adequate force commanded by the most competent officer in America for such service, General N. B. Forrest, could be sent . . . for the purpose of breaking the railroad in Sherman's rear"; and he "made the suggestion direct to the President."

Forrest had already been at work behind Sherman. When, in February, Sooy Smith had brought a Union force south from Memphis to locate and neutralize him, the raw-boned Southerner soon had him headed north again in "a weary, disheartened, almost panic-stricken flight, in the greatest disorder." In May Sherman had sent Brigadier General S. D. Sturgis, supported by 3400 cavalry under Grierson, into northern Mississippi to forestall a descent by Forrest on his line of communications. But at Brice's Crossroads on June 10 an all-day fight ended in a Federal defeat that was owing largely to Forrest's flanking movement and the accurate fire of his artillery. "At first sullenly," Adjutant General Roger W. Hanson recalled, "and then rapidly, the whole line fell back. . . . Utter disorganization succeeded disorder [which lasted] all through the night . . . reaching Ripley, 24 miles from the field, by early morning. It con-

195

Blockhouse on the Tennessee River.

Gen. James R. Chalmers, C.S.A.

196

tinued to Memphis. . . . There was no success among the many won by Forrest comparable to that."

President Davis instructed General Richard Taylor, commanding the Department of Alabama, Mississippi, and East Louisiana, to employ Forrest "to interfere with supplies and reinforcements" being forwarded to Sherman. Taylor, who had never seen Forrest before, found him "a tall, stalwart man, with grayish hair, a mild countenance and slow and homely speech." But upon getting the information he needed, "Forrest's whole manner now changed. In a dozen sharp sentences he told his wants . . . informed me he would march with the dawn."

North of the Tennessee, on September 23, the appearance of his horsemen was so sudden and unexpected that the blockhouses and garrison at Athens, Alabama, "found them-

Jefferson Davis, President of the Confederacy.

Railroad yards at Chattanooga, Tenn.

Country made to order for attacks on Sherman's supply lines. The road
through Running Water Creek Gap, ten miles west of Chattanooga.

selves hopelessly corralled"; and once more employing his trick of magnifying his forces, he received the surrender of 1300 Federals. He dispatched James Chalmers's division west, toward Memphis to destroy all trestles and himself headed north, "tearing up the track and capturing blockhouses" as he went.

Sherman telegraphed to Grant: "Can't you expedite the sending to Nashville of recruits that are in Indiana and Ohio? Forrest is now lieutenant-general and commands all . . . cavalry." Forrest shoved Major General L. H. Rousseau's reinforcements into Pulaski and turned east as troop trains shuttled the Federals through Nashville to meet the new threat. Major General Robert Milroy, who had been beaten by Stonewall Jackson's foot

Gen. Robert H. Milroy, U.S.A.

Sullivan's Branch No. 2 on the Northwestern Railroad, connecting Johnsonville with Nashville. Wooden trestles such as those here invited destruction by raiders.

cavalry in the Shenandoah Valley in 1862, found himself again frustrated. He reported from Tullahoma: "I confidently expected an attack . . . but to my great disappointment and disgust they failed to come, and my preparations for meeting them were useless." Sherman grumbled to the War Department that Forrest's cavalry would "travel 100 miles in less time than ours will ten. . . . Keep Forrest away from me, and I will . . . cut the Confederacy in two."

After slipping back into northern Alabama to shake off pursuit and replenish his ammunition, in October Forrest swept into western Tennessee, captured a transport on the Tennessee River, and from its cargo was able to issue badly needed new clothes to his men. One of Chalmers's detachments captured the

transport *Venus,* and shortly took over the gunboat *Undine.* Forrest decided to put crews of "horse marines" aboard both these vessels and with their support to attack the Federal supply base at Johnsonville. "I promise not to haul you over the coals if you come home wet," he assured his somewhat dubious commodore. It was a promise that soon required fulfillment, for Union gunboats quickly eliminated his fleet.

Opposite Johnsonville he found "the whole wharf lined with transports and gunboats . . . an immense warehouse [and] several acres of the shore . . . covered with every description of army stores." He opened fire on this conglomeration of targets late in the afternoon, and although fifty Federal guns replied, gunboats, transports, and the piles of supplies were

Forrest found the Federal supply depot at Johnsonville a rich plum. He estimated that he destroyed nearly seven million dollars worth of Sherman's supplies here.

The railroad yards at Nashville were busy with Federal troop trains.

soon ablaze. "By night the wharf for nearly one mile up and down the river presented one solid sheet of flame"; and the Federal Assistant Inspector General complained: "On the evening of the fire the railroad agent . . . ran off with a train of cars loaded with clothing and some 400 men from gunboats. . . . Twelve miles from Johnsonville he detached the engine and tender and went to Nashville." Back in Corinth again by November 10, Forrest figured that at the expense of a dozen casualties he had destroyed eighteen boats and close to $7,000,000 worth of Sherman's supplies.

But it was all too late. It had been impos-

sible for the Confederate army commanders to follow Forrest's dictum and "Get there first with the most men." Atlanta was in ashes, and Sherman was marching to the sea. New blood had been pumped down to him for the final round. Kilpatrick had been riding for him since April, butting heads with Joe Wheeler all the way to Atlanta, and with his compatriots between fights. Sherman thought him "a crazy damn fool," but he was getting the job done.

James Wilson was ordered down to command the cavalry in the march to the sea. But after conferring with Sherman, he found himself lacking 4500 horses and was assigned to

The Capitol at Nashville.

duty under Thomas at Nashville. It was a fortunate move. By December Wilson had helped General John M. Schofield defeat Hood at Franklin and had set about building a cavalry corps in northern Alabama. Never had such a formidable body of cavalry been assembled in the New World. It numbered 16,000 men, and most of them were armed with the Spencer repeating carbine.

Forrest could not hope to match it. "The horse supply was the weakest point of all the organization of [our] cavalry," a Confederate officer explained. "When a man enlisted he brought with him his own mount. If dismounted he must provide himself with another horse, or be transferred to another branch of the service. Good men were often lost." Stables had been swept clean of horses all over the South. A Southern girl wrote in her diary that winter: "When the call for horses was made, Mrs. McCord sent her fine bays. She comes now with a pair of mules and looks too long at my ponies." Mrs. Jefferson Davis found that she could not keep her horses, could not feed them. But that was in Richmond, where the price of oats, like that of everything else, had become exorbitant.

Many of the distinguished cavalry leaders were gone, too: not only Jeb Stuart, but less famous men such as Chambliss and other field officers whose skill and daring had made the exploits of the Confederate cavalry possible. Now a South Carolina newspaper announced: "They say General Morgan has been killed." It was true. The Kentucky cavalier had burrowed out of his Ohio cell in November, 1863, to receive a hero's welcome in Richmond. While he was rebuilding a command near Atlanta the following February the mayor had given him a royal reception at the Trout House. But a summer raid into Kentucky had

backfired, and that September saw him driven into Greenville, Tennessee, and his headquarters surrounded by Federal soldiers under the command of Brigadier General A. C. Gillem.

There was a demand that Morgan surrender, one of his men reported, and cries of "Kill him! . . . I saw General Morgan throw up his hands, exclaiming, 'Oh, God!' . . . He was brought to the street dead." It remained for Joe Wheeler and Wade Hampton, with weary men and worn-down horses, to keep the flag of the Confederate cavalry flying.

As Sherman marched northward from Savannah in January, 1865, with Kilpatrick's

Morgan, who had escaped from his Ohio prison and was rebuilding his command near Atlanta, was given a royal reception at the Trout House there.

troopers clearing the way, "Kill Cavalry" boasted of his intentions when he reached South Carolina: "There'll be damn little for you infantrymen to destroy after I've passed through that hellhole of secession." And a Federal chaplain observed that he "fitted all the boys' saddlebags with matches before leaving Savannah." It was not an inaccurate indication of their future actions, although some of the wealthy planters burned their own houses rather than have them "polluted" by the presence of the Yankees in them. "Sometimes the world seemed on fire," wrote one veteran of that march. "We were almost stifled by smoke and flames."

Early in March, Wheeler and his men swam the swollen Peedee River to meet them. Co-operating closely with Wade Hampton's troop-

Gen. Alvan C. Gillem, U.S.A.

204

Listening to the violin. Rare tintype of unidentified cavalrymen in camp.

Columbia, South Carolina, shown here from the capitol, was in ruins after Sherman passed through it.

ers, he charged into the Federal camp at the crack of dawn on the 9th. "In less than a minute," a shocked Kilpatrick recorded, they "had driven back my people and taken possession." He called it "the most formidable cavalry charge I ever have witnessed." He himself escaped only by sprinting into the pines. But stragglers from both armies were robbing and ravaging over the country, calling themselves "Wheeler's men"; and General Beauregard, as super-departmental commander of the Military Division of the West, recommended that Wade Hampton replace Wheeler as chief of cavalry, on the ground that Wheeler, "though modest, zealous, gallant and indefatigable," could not "properly control and direct . . . a corps of cavalry."

The superseded "banty" took the humiliation with a smile. "I will receive your orders with pleasure," he told Hampton. But even cheerful self-abnegation availed little now. In mid-February Sherman had left South Carolina's capital burning. By March 10 he was at Fayetteville, in North Carolina, and the Carolina railroads were ruined. Sheridan was cutting through Virginia's hinterland again; George Stoneman was raiding eastward out of Tennessee; and late in March Wilson's force began moving in the farther South, brushing aside Forrest's opposition. From Elyton (Birmingham), Wilson sent John Croxton west to Tuscaloosa to burn the University, which he rated as a "military school," since it had a cadet corps. A futile attempt to stop Wilson's cavalry was made at Montevallo, on the last day of March, and a two-day running fight ended at Selma, where Forrest was pushed back to Gainesville.

205

Gen. Joseph E. Johnston, C.S.A.

17

Federal Cavalry Guidon.

The Horsemen in at the Death

IN THE RICHMOND-PETERSBURG country a grim and dreary winter grew grimmer and more dreary still as the spring of 1865 approached. With Christmas the bad news had begun to pour in: Savannah taken; Hood defeated at Nashville, and his army practically destroyed; Fort Fisher stormed in January; Wilmington, that handy port for blockade-runners, lost; and Charleston surrendered in February.

Sheridan's horsemen had swept the valley of the upper James clear of provender. One time in January there was only a two days' supply of rations for the Confederate men in the Petersburg trenches; and in February Lee appealed to the country directly for supplies for his half-starved soldiers, who were ragged and mostly barefoot. Even munitions were so scarce that, while a collection of lead fruit-jar covers was being made in Richmond, the soldiers dug spent bullets out of the earth to fire back at an enemy whose ammunition appeared to be unlimited. As time went on, more of them drifted across the picket lines under cover of darkness to become the willing prisoners of the Federal troops. There was little fighting spirit left among Richmond's civilians. The Clerks' Battalion shrank from 700 to 200 men, and other home defense organizations were equally depleted.

207

Interior of Fort Stedman, Petersburg. Grant claimed he took 2000 prisoners here.

Fodder was so scarce that the field artillery had to keep their horses too far away for their guns to be efficient at a sudden call. In the cavalry there was an increasing dearth of horses; and none had come in from either of the Carolinas in response to the government's call to those states for re-mounts. Yet Fitzhugh Lee must contrive somehow to combat Sheridan's numerous, well-armed, and well-mounted cavalry, with which Grant kept reaching west and southward to sever the South Side Railroad, Lee's army's life-line. Behind the cavalry marched the Federal infantry and guns, digging in as they came, until Lee, with but 57,000, must strive to hold a line thirty-five miles long against Grant's 125,000 men.

Capt. John C. Calhoun, 4th South Carolina Cavalry, C.S.A

A brigade of Sheridan's cavalry, commanded by Gen. Henry E. Davies, JR., intercepted a wagon train and artillery at Paine's Crossroads, near Jetersville, on April 5, 1865. Sheridan reported to Grant that 200 wagons, five pieces of artillery, and eight or nine battle flags were taken. "I see no escape for Lee," Sheridan wrote.

209

Horses of Federal cavalrymen are hitched to a fence in Richmond.

Soon after the beginning of the year, Rear Admiral Raphael Semmes returned from three years of activity in which his cruisers had been a terror to Union commerce. He spent a night at Lee's headquarters at the Turnbull house, two miles west of Petersburg. He had already dined at the Executive Mansion, where the President had talked with an obstinate optimism, though Mrs. Davis made it clear that she had no hope of the future of the Confederacy. Semmes found Lee frankly and absolutely without hope of winning the war. No man, Lee said, could save the country now; the body politic was dead.

Lee, at long last, had been made commander-in-chief of all the armies of the Confederacy. He sent Joseph Johnston to the Carolinas to collect and lead the scattered Confederate forces in those parts against Sherman's advancing army. In combats that raged from the 19th of March to the 21st at Bentonville, Johnston was defeated. A little earlier that month Richmond was startled by the news that Sheridan's squadrons were at Gordonsville and Scotsville, heading for the South Side Railroad. At one in the morning of March 12 the sound of the tocsin threw the city into a panic with a false report that Sheridan was at the western fortifications. It was said that President Davis and members of his cabinet had their horses saddled for flight. Between 1000 and 1500 Federal horsemen had indeed advanced toward the city but had fallen back when they met with opposition.

On March 25 came the capture and loss of Fort Stedman by Early's old corps, which cost Lee's army, Grant claimed, 2000 men in prisoners. Four days later Grant struck with Sheridan's cavalry at Burkeville, where the South Side and the Richmond and Danville railroads intersect. Fitzhugh Lee's horsemen, supported by Pickett's and Johnson's infantry, drove him back to Dinwiddie Court House. But the next day, April 1, Sheridan, reinforced by the Fed-

eral Sixth Corps, assaulted Pickett and defeated him at Five Forks.

It was the final blow to the defense of Petersburg. Unless Lee chose to be surrounded and starved into surrender, he must escape and join Johnston's army in North Carolina. The next day Federal troops broke the line of fortifications on the Confederate right; and that same night the Army of Northern Virginia evacuated their redoubts and trenches at Petersburg and Richmond and started westward.

At dawn the next day the cavalry of the rear guard trotted across Mayo's Bridge to Manchester, passed the railroad station, which was thronged with fugitives vainly waiting for a

The residence of President Jefferson Davis attracts curious Union soldiers.

train, and took the road that was to lead them to Appomattox. They had hardly disappeared before Union cavalry trotted up Richmond's Broad Street and wheeled through the iron gates into Capitol Square. Down came the Stars and Bars and the long blue banner of Virginia, and up over Thomas Jefferson's Roman replica went the Stars and Stripes to the strains of the "Star-Spangled Banner."

Lee aimed at the Danville Railroad, intending to reach either Danville or Lynchburg and unite with Johnston. But the provisions that he had arranged to have awaiting his army at Amelia Court House had been mis-sent to Richmond, and he lost twenty-four priceless hours in trying to collect subsistence for his men and horses from the surrounding country.

Soon Union columns were on his left flank and rear; and Sheridan's cavalry, riding far ahead, turned Lee away from Burkes Station on the Danville Railroad. On April 6 his rear guard, some 8000 strong, was surrounded and captured. For four days his men had had nothing to eat but a little parched corn. He crossed to the north side of the Appomattox, burning the bridges behind him. But the Federal troops saved one of them and were soon at his heels again. His new rear guard beat them off; but at Appomattox Court House he found Sheridan blocking his further retreat. On April 9 he surrendered—28,000 men, all that were left to him. Two divisions of his cavalry, under General T. L. Rosser, had burst through the encircling enemy and escaped to Lynchburg.

News of Lee's surrender found Johnston's army near Durham's Station, in North Carolina, not far from the Virginia line, with his cavalry, under Wade Hampton and Wheeler, screening his front and flanks from Sherman's army, which recent reinforcements had increased to 80,000. The campaigning of the past weeks had terribly weakened Johnston's army; desertion had been rife; and he had been compelled to send off a detachment to cope with a raid of Federal cavalry from Tennessee into western North Carolina.

A review that he held early in April revealed the discouraging fact that he could muster only 29,000 men. Many of his regiments were represented by only thirty or forty enlisted men. Their clothing and shoes—when they were not barefoot—were deplorable. Arms and equipment had suffered severely from the attrition of months of service in which there had been no adequate replacements. Their commander's one hope of keeping the war going had been the plan of union with Lee; and with the news of Appomattox that vanished. Surrender on the best terms obtainable was the only course left open to him, as he saw clearly. To continue fighting on would be little short of mass murder, an abominable injustice to the gallant men who had stayed with him. Even the fiery Beauregard agreed with him.

But President Davis, who had made good his flight from Richmond by special train to Danville and had lately arrived at nearby Greensboro, saw it otherwise. Upon the news of Lee's surrender Davis had resumed command of the armies of the Confederacy. With an obstinate optimism that amounted to pigheadedness, he summoned Johnston and Beauregard to Greensboro and laid before them a fantastic scheme of marching to Texas and, with Texas as a base and Mexico as a source of supplies, carrying on the war. The two generals promptly and frankly condemned the plan as an impossibility. The war was over, they told him. They welcomed Sherman's offer to accept the surrender of Johnston's army on the same terms that Grant had given Lee, "pure and simple": all arms to be surrendered; officers and men alike to sign written promises that they would not bear arms against the Federal government again; private horses to be retained by their owners; officers to keep their side arms and to be allowed wagons to take their personal property home with them.

212

News of President Lincoln's assassination raised some doubts as to whether these terms would be approved at Washington. But after several days of haggling over details the surrender was carried through on these lines. May 2 and 3 were taken up with the signing of the written promises, though many men quietly took their departure before their turn came to sign, and on the latter date Johnston's army ceased to exist.

For Wade Hampton and Wheeler the pill was too bitter to be swallowed, so bitter that Jefferson Davis's mad Texas project seemed sweet by comparison. On the grounds that they were at Greensboro, directly under Davis's orders, on the day the surrender was signed, they refused to be bound by it. Wheeler quickly collected 600 volunteers from his own regiments and rode off with them to join his President. Some hundreds of Hampton's troopers, stirred by this example, saddled up and rode away, swearing that the war was not over so far as they were concerned. Hampton sent them stern orders to return, galloped after

213

Custer receives Lee's flag of truce at Appomattox. Sheridan later gave the flag to Custer as a present. "I know of no one," Sheridan wrote, "whose efforts have contributed more to this happy result."

them, and, overtaking them at sunrise next day, explained to them that while he had not been included in the surrender, they were in honor bound to abide by it. Their officers passed the word among them: the war was over; their well-loved commander ordered them to assemble at Greensboro and give up.

Riding on with a small party in an effort to overtake President Davis, who was heading for the unsurrendered Confederate troops in Alabama, with Union cavalry at his heels, Hampton reached his old home at Yorkville in South Carolina. His wife was there to receive him,

and Wheeler, too. Together they persuaded Hampton that it would be futile for him, in his exhausted physical condition, to attempt to join the president.

Wheeler, whose command had been steadily dwindling, now broke it up into small parties, the better to elude capture, and pressed on after Davis, who, finally aware of the complete collapse of the Confederacy, was heading for Florida and escape. At Washington, Georgia, Wheeler learned that Davis had disbanded the troops that had formed his escort; and he gathered that his own escape had now better

President Davis, captured in the pine forests of Georgia, is conveyed through Macon in an ambulance.

214

In Washington, Union cavalry participated in the grand review of the Army.

be his chief concern. The woods were full of parties searching for him. A few days later he and the few that remained with him were surprised and captured while they slept the sleep of utter exhaustion. He was taken to Athens, Georgia, where he was added to the distinguished group of prisoners that included Jefferson Davis and several others who had shared his flight. There would be some months in the dungeons of Fort Delaware before "Fightin'

Joe" Wheeler breathed the air of freedom again.

So much for the Horsemen in Gray. For the Horsemen in Blue, there was the parade down Pennsylvania Avenue, to the blare and thunder of their bands. The troopers of Sheridan and Kilpatrick were acclaimed with a joyous enthusiasm that even sorrow for a murdered President could not lessen.

215

Acknowledgments

The following Historical Societies, Libraries, Museums and Institutions have contributed pictorial material and help in other ways, which is gratefully acknowledged:

Carnegie Library of Rome, Georgia (Mrs. J. L. Henderson)

Chicago Historical Society, Chicago, Illinois (Mr. Paul Angle and Mrs. Paul M. Rymer)

Confederate Museum, Richmond, Virginia (Miss India Thomas and Miss Eleanor Brockenbrough)

Cooper Union Museum for the Arts of Decoration, New York, New York (Mr. Maurice Block)

Corcoran Gallery of Art, Washington, D.C. (Mr. Horace Hotchkiss, Jr.)

The Filson Club, Louisville, Kentucky

Fredericksburg & Spotsylvania National Military Park, Fredericksburg, Virginia (Mr. Albert Dillahunty, Mr. Ralph Happel, and Mr. Robert L. Hilldrup)

Gadsden Public Library, Gadsden, Alabama (Miss Lena Martin)

The Handley Library, Winchester, Virginia (Mr. Vernon Eddy)

The Hunt-Morgan House, Lexington, Kentucky (Mrs. Julian Elliott)

Illinois State Historical Library, Springfield, Illinois (Mrs. Margaret A. Flint and Mr. Clyde C. Walton)

The Indianapolis Public Library, Indianapolis, Indiana

Kansas State Historical Society, Topeka, Kansas (Mr. Robert W. Richmond)

Kentucky Historical Society, Frankfort, Kentucky

The Library of Congress, Washington, D.C. (Dr. Edgar Breitenbach, Mr. Milton Kaplan, Mr. Frederick R. Goff, Mr. Jerome M. Edelstein, Mr. Richard S. Hill, and Mr. Oliver A. Dudley)

Minnesota Historical Society, St. Paul, Minnesota (Miss Bertha L. Heilbron and Mr. Eugene D. Becker)

Missouri Historical Society, St. Louis, Missouri (Mrs. Marjory Douglas and Miss Ruth Field)

The National Archives, Washington, D.C. (Miss Josephine Cobb, Mr. Elmer O. Parker, and Mr. Julio Perez)

New-York Historical Society, New York, New York (Mr. Arthur B. Carlson)

Smithsonian Institution, Washington, D.C. (Mr. Edgar Howell, and Mr. Craddock Goins, Jr.)

New York Public Library, New York, New York (Miss Elizabeth Roth)

Texas History Center, University of Texas, Austin, Texas (Miss Llerena B. Friend)

The University of Kansas Library, Lawrence, Kansas

The University of Louisville Library, Louisville, Kentucky (Margaret Bridwell)

University of North Carolina Library, Chapel Hall, N. C. (Mr. James W. Patton)

The Valentine Museum, Richmond, Virginia (Mrs. Ralph Catterall and Miss Elizabeth J. Dance)

West Point Museum, United States Military Academy, West Point, New York (Mr. Richard E. Kuehne)

Witte Memorial Museum, San Antonio, Texas (Miss Eleana Onderdonk and Mr. Charles J. Long)

217

The generous help of the following is acknowledged:

Miss Josephine Cobb, Archivist-in-charge of the Still Picture Branch, The National Archives, whose knowledge of Civil War photographs made our task of selection and identification less difficult and her efficient staff: Mrs. Ruth King, Miss Josephine Motylewski, Mr. Joe Thomas, and Mr. Harry Bauda.

Mr. Donald Holmes, Chief of the Photoduplication Service, Library of Congress and the following members of his staff: Mr. William E. Davis, Mr. Elmer King, Mrs. Ernestine B. Jacobs, Mrs. Virginia Brooks, Miss Olivera Durgy, Mr. Edward J. Brocious, Mr. Harrison Allen, and Mr. Vincent J. Puccio. Without their skill and patience it would have been impossible to reproduce many of the pictures used.

Miss India Thomas, House Regent, and Miss Eleanor Brockenbrough, Assistant House Regent, Confederate Museum, Richmond, Virginia, were extremely kind and helpful and supplied a number of important photographs from their notable collection.

Mrs. Ralph Catterall, Librarian, and Miss Elizabeth J. Dance, Assistant Librarian, The Valentine Museum, Richmond, Virginia, for their invaluable assistance and making available certain rare photographs in the Cook Collection.

Mr. and Mrs. Edgar Cox, Falls Church, Virginia, for granting permission to reproduce certain photographs in the Brady-Handy Collection in the Library of Congress.

Special acknowledgment is due Mr. Lee Grove, Pearl River, New York, for his encouragement and guidance in the early stages of this work and his creative skill in the preparation of the picture captions.

Among others to whom the authors are deeply indebted are:

Mr. Rucker Agee, Birmingham, Alabama

Mr. Ben Belchic, Winchester, Virginia

Mr. Charles Bell, Louisville, Kentucky

Dr. Carl Bogardus, Austin, Indiana

Mr. Carl Breihan, St. Louis, Missouri

Mrs. Peel Cannon, Holly Springs, Mississippi

Miss Anne Carper, Herndon, Virginia

Mr. G. Glenn Clift, Frankfort, Kentucky

Dr. Allen Crafton, Lawrence, Kansas

Judge William Finley, Falls Church, Virginia

Mr. Craddock Goins, Jr., Arlington, Virginia

Mrs. Frank Hammond, Springfield, Virginia

Mr. James Harriman, Louisville, Kentucky

Mr. Henry C. Hastings, Lawrence, Kansas

Miss Lillian Heckel, Louisville, Kentucky

Mr. Richard Hill, Louisville, Kentucky

Miss Mary E. Hinds, Manhattan, Kansas

Mr. Gouverneur Hoes, Washington, D.C.

Mr. Edgar Howell, Falls Church, Virginia

Mrs. Mabel Huckaby, Austin, Texas

Mr. J. Marvin Hunter, Sr., Bandera, Texas

Mr. Asa Moore Janney, Lincoln, Virginia

Colonel G. B. Jarrett, Aberdeen, Maryland

Miss Betty Ann Johnson, Norfolk, Virginia

Mr. Ralph P. Johnson, Osceola, Missouri

Mrs. Varina R. Jones, Alexandria, Virginia

Mr. Virgil C. Jones, Centerville, Virginia

Mrs. McCook Knox, Washington, D.C.

Mrs. J. S. Land, Columbia, South Carolina

Mr. Hugo H. Loewenstern, Amarillo, Texas

Mr. Edward McArtor, Lakeland, Florida

Mr. Bernard McCarthy, Washington, D.C.

Miss Helen M. McFarland, Topeka, Missouri

Mr. Anson T. McCook, Hartford, Connecticut

Miss Frances McCook, Hartford, Connecticut

Mr. Rex Magee, Arlington, Virginia

Mr. Julien D. Martin, Wilmington, North Carolina

Dr. and Mrs. Daniel B. Moffett, Washington, D.C.

Mr. Van L. Naisawald, Manassas, Virginia

Mr. Curtis Oaks, Taylorsville, Kentucky

Miss Alice Lee Parker, Washington, D.C.

Mr. John R. Peacock, High Point, North Carolina

Mr. Harold Petersen, Arlington, Virginia

Mrs. J. Garnet Petersen, San Antonio, Texas

Mrs. Fletcher Plumley, Washington, D.C.

Mr. John Rawls, Vienna, Virginia

Mr. Robert G. Sanner, Manassas, Virginia

Mr. Melvin M. Scott, Falls Church, Virginia

Mr. Thomas Shaw, Falls Church, Virginia

Dr. Hambleton Tapp, Lexington, Kentucky

Mr. William H. Townsend, Louisville, Kentucky

Mr. Tom Wallace, Louisville, Kentucky

Mr. Ezra J. Warner, La Jolla, California

Mr. William Weise, Quantico, Virginia

Mr. E. B. White, Leesburg, Virginia

Mr. Francis F. Wilshin, Manassas, Virginia

Mr. Landon Wynkoop, Leesburg, Virginia

Mr. B. E. Young, Washington, D.C.

Dr. Harold Young, Washington, D.C.

Thanks are due to the publishers from whom permissions
to quote have been received:

American Heritage and Indiana University Press for "A
Visit to Civil War America," by C. F. Pisani, published
by the Indiana University Press as *Prince Napoleon in
America, 1861.*

Houghton Mifflin Company for *A Diary from Dixie,* Mary
Boykin Chesnut.

University of Illinois Press, *Grierson's Raid,* D. Alexander
Brown; *The Civil War Letters of Sergeant Olney Andrus,* F. A. Shannon.

Kentucky Historical Society, *Register of the,* July, 1935.

Alfred A. Knopf, *The General Who Marched to Hell,* Earl S.
Miers.

Louisiana State University Press, *Fightin' Joe Wheeler,*
John P. Dyer.

J. B. Lippincott Company, *Lieutenant General Jubal Anderson Early,* by J. E. Early.

Little, Brown & Company, *Meade's Headquarters,* Theodore Lyman.

University of North Carolina, *Rustics in Rebellion,* George
Alfred Townsend.

University of Pittsburgh, *The North Reports the Civil War,*
by J. Cutler Andrews.

Charles Scribner's Sons, *Letters from Lee's Army,* C. M.
Blackford III; *War Years with Jeb Stuart,* W. W. Blackford; *J.E.B. Stuart,* John W. Thomason, Jr.

Yale University Press, *A Volunteer's Adventures,* J. W. De-
Forrest.

Bibliography

American Heritage, August 1957.

American Historical Association Report, 1894.

Andrews, J. C.: *The North Reports the Civil War,* Pittsburgh, 1955.

Appler, A. C.: *The Younger Brothers,* New York, 1955.

Battles and Leaders of the Civil War, New York, 1884.

Behn, George W.: *A Concise System of Instruction for the Volunteer Cavalry of the United States,* Savannah, 1842.

Bickham, W. D.: *Rosecrans' Campaign with the Fourteenth Army Corps,* Cincinnati, 1863.

Bill, A. H.: *The Beleaguered City,* New York, 1946.

Binney, C. C.: *The Life of Horace Binney,* Philadelphia, 1903.

Black, Robert C., III: *The Railroads of the Confederacy,* Chapel Hill, 1952.

Blackford, C. M., III (edited by): *Letters from Lee's Army,* New York, 1947.

Blackford, W. W.: *War Years with JEB Stuart,* New York, 1946.

Borcke, Heros von: *Memoirs of the Confederate War,* New York, 1938.

Bowman, Col. S. M. & Lt. Col. R. B. Irwin: *Sherman and His Campaigns,* New York, 1865.

Brown, Alexander D.: *Grierson's Raid,* Urbana, Ill., 1954.

Burch, J. P.: *Charles W. Quantrell,* Kansas City, Kans., 1923.

Chesnut, Mary Boykin: *A Diary from Dixie* (Ed. Ben Ames Williams), Boston, 1949.

Century Magazine, May 1898, New York.

Chicago Tribune, July 30, 1863.

Commager, Henry S.: *The Blue and the Gray,* Indianapolis, 1950.

Connelly, W. E.: *Quantrill and the Border Wars,* Cedar Rapids, 1910.

Cooke, John Esten: *Wearing of the Gray,* New York, 1867.

Crafton, Allen: *Free State Fortress,* Lawrence, Kans., 1954.

Crawford, J. M.: *Mosby and His Men,* New York, 1867.

Croffut, W. A.: *An American Procession,* Boston, 1931.

Cullum, George W.: *Biographical Register of Officers and Graduates of the United States Military Academy,* Boston, 1891.

Custer, Elizabeth B.: *Tenting on the Plains,* New York, 1893.

Davis, Jefferson: *A Short History of the Confederate States of America,* New York, 1890.

Davis, Mrs. Jefferson: *Jefferson Davis, Ex-President of the Confederate States* (vol. 2), New York, 1890.

DeForest, William, Jr.: *A Volunteer's Adventures* (Ed. J. H. Croushore), New Haven, 1946.

Dyer, John Will: *Reminiscences, Four Years in the Confederate Army,* Evansville, Ind., 1898.

Dyer, John P.: *"Fightin' Joe" Wheeler,* Baton Rouge, 1941.

Early, J. A.: *Lieutenant General Jubal Anderson Early,* Philadelphia, 1912.

Forrest, N. B.: *Testimony Before 42nd Congress, 1872, 2nd Session, Senate Document,* No. 41, Vol. 13.

Freeman, Douglas S.: *Lee's Lieutenants* (3 vols.), New York, 1942, 1943, 1944.

Gilmore, J. R.: *Personal Recollections of Abraham Lincoln and the Civil War,* Boston, 1898.

Goss, W. L.: *Recollections of a Private, a Story of the Army of the Potomac,* New York, 1890.

Grant, U. S.: *Personal Memories of U. S. Grant,* New York, 1895.

Gray, Capt. Alonzo: *Cavalry Tactics,* Fort Leavenworth, Kans., 1910.

Guild, George B.: *A Brief Narrative of the Fourth Tennessee Cavalry Regiment,* Nashville, 1913.

Harper's Pictorial History of the Civil War, Star Series, Vol. II, Chicago, 1866–68.

Hartpence, Sergeant Major Wm. R.: *History of the 51st Indiana Veteran Infantry,* Indianapolis, 1894.

Henry, R. S.: *"First with the Most Forrest,"* Indianapolis, 1944.

Henry, R. S.: *The Story of the Confederacy,* New York, 1931.

Holland, C. F.: *Morgan and His Raiders,* New York, 1942.

Horn, S. F.: *The Army of Tennessee,* Indianapolis, 1941.

Illinois State Historical Society, Transactions of, for the Year 1928 (Letters of Major Austin Connolly), Springfield, 1928.

Johnson, Brig. Gen. A. R.: *The Partisan Rangers of the Confederate States Army,* Louisville, 1904.

Johnson, Byron Berkley: *Abraham Lincoln and Boston Corbett,* Waltham, Mass., 1914.

Jones, J. B.: *A Rebel War Clerk's Diary,* Philadelphia, 1866.

Jones, V. C.: *Ranger Mosby,* Chapel Hill, 1944.

Kentucky State Historical Society, Register of the, July 1935, Frankfort, Ky.

Lyman, Colonel Theodore: *Meade's Headquarters, 1863–1865,* Boston, 1922.

Mansfield, E. D.: *The Mexican War, A History of Its Origin,* New York, 1850.

Maury, D. H.: *Recollections of a Virginian,* New York, 1897.

McClellan, H. B.: *The Life and Campaigns of Major General J. E. B. Stuart,* Boston, 1885.

Miers, Earl S.: *The General Who Marched to Hell,* New York, 1951.

Miller, F. T.: *The Photographic History of the Civil War,* New York, 1912.

Moore, Frank: *The Civil War in Song and Story,* New York, 1887.

Munson, John W.: *Reminiscences of a Mosby Guerrilla,* Boston, 1906.

Nichols, George Ward: *The Story of the Great March,* New York, 1865.

Official Records of the Union and Confederate Armies, Washington, 1880–1901.

O'Flaherty, Daniel: *General Jo Shelby,* Chapel Hill, 1954.

Owsley, Frank Lawrence: *State Rights in the Confederacy,* Chicago, 1925.

Peck, W. F. G.: "Four Years under Fire at Charleston," *Harper's Monthly Magazine,* XXXI, 1865.

Pemberton, John C.: *Pemberton, Defender of Vicksburg,* Chapel Hill, 1942.

Piatt, Don: *Memories of the Men Who Saved the Union,* New York, 1887.

Pratt, Fletcher: *Ordeal by Fire,* New York, 1935.

Pratt, Fletcher: *Stanton, Lincoln's Secretary of War,* New York, 1953.

Prentice Press: *The Confederate Soldier in the Civil War,* Louisville, 1897.

Register of the Kentucky State Historical Society, July 1935.

Roach, Lt. A. C.: *The Prisoner of War and How Treated,* Indianapolis, 1865.

Ropes, John C.: *The Story of the Civil War,* New York, 1894–1913.

Russell, William Howard, *My Diary, North and South* (Ed. Fletcher Pratt), New York, 1954; also London, 1863.

Schofield, Lt. Gen. J. M.: *Forty-six Years in the Army,* New York, 1897.

Scott, John: *Partisan Life with Mosby,* London, 1867.

Shannon, F. A.: *The Civil War Letters of Sergeant Onley Andrus,* Urbana, 1947.

Sherman, W. T.: *Memoirs of General William T. Sherman,* Vol. 2., New York, 1875.

Sheridan, Lt. Gen., Philip H.: *Personal Memoirs of,* New York, 1888.

Steele, M. F.: *American Campaigns,* Harrisburg, Pa., 1949.

Stiles, R. S.: *Four Years under Marse Lee,* New York, 1904.

Taylor, Lt. Gen. Richard, C.S.A.: *Destruction and Reconstruction,* New York, 1879.

Thomason, John W., Jr.: *JEB Stuart,* New York, 1934.

Thorndike, Rachel Sherman (ed.): *The Sherman Letters,* New York, 1894.

Townsend, George Alfred: *Rustics in Rebellion,* Chapel Hill, 1950.

Wellman, Manly Wade: *Giant in Gray,* New York, 1949.

Wells, E. D.: *Hampton and His Cavalry in 1864,* Richmond, 1899.

Wyeth, J. A.: *Life of General Nathan Bedford Forrest,* New York, 1901.

Young, B. H.: *Confederate Wizards of the Saddle,* Boston, 1914.

Picture Sources

PAGE

ii Drawing by Winslow Homer, 1863. Collection, Cooper Union Museum for the Arts of Decoration, New York, N.Y.

2 *Left:* Photograph by Mathew B. Brady. Collection, Library of Congress, Washington, D.C.
Right: Photograph. Collection, Library of Congress.

3 *Top:* Drawing by Alfred R. Waud. Collection, Library of Congress.
Bottom: Broadside. Collection, Mr. Hugh H. Loewenstern, Amarillo, Texas.

4 Drawing by Alfred R. Waud. Collection, Library of Congress.

5 Drawing by Alfred R. Waud. Collection, Library of Congress.

6 *Top:* Ambrotype. Collection, Mrs. Fletcher Plumley, Washington, D.C.
Bottom: Collection, Smithsonian Institution, Washington, D.C.

7 *Top:* Drawing by Alfred R. Waud. Collection, Library of Congress
Bottom: Collection, Music Division, Library of Congress.

8 *Top:* Photograph by Joel E. Whitney, St. Paul, Minnesota. Collection, Minnesota Historical Society, St. Paul.
Bottom: Drawing by Alfred R. Waud. Collection, Library of Congress.

9 Wood-engraving, *Harper's Weekly,* 1861. Collection, Library of Congress.

10 Photograph by Mathew B. Brady, Collection, Library of Congress.

11 Photographs by Mathew B. Brady. Collection, Library of Congress.

12 Photographs by Mathew B. Brady. Collection, Library of Congress.

13 Ambrotype. Collection, Mr. Thomas Shaw, Falls Church, Virginia.

14 *Left:* Ambrotype. Collection, Confederate Museum, Richmond, Va.
Right: Ambrotype. Collection, Miss Anne Carper, Herndon, Va.

15 *Left:* Ambrotype. Collection, Confederate Museum, Richmond, Va.
Right: Ambrotype. Collection, Confederate Museum, Richmond, Va.

16 Photograph. Cook Collection, Valentine Museum, Richmond, Va.

17 Collection, Confederate Museum, Richmond, Va.

18 Ambrotype. Collection, Confederate Museum, Richmond, Va.

19 *Top:* Photograph by James F. Gibson. Collection, Library of Congress.
Bottom: Photograph. Cook Collection, Valentine Museum, Richmond, Va.

20 *Top:* Photograph. Collection, National Archives, Washington, D.C.
Bottom: Photograph by Mathew B. Brady. Brady-Handy Collection, Library of Congress.

21 Wood-engraving. *New York Illustrated News,* 1862. Collection, Library of Congress.

22 *Top:* Photograph by Mathew B. Brady. Collection, National Archives.
Bottom: Map by James R. Johnson.

23 *Top:* Photograph by James F. Gibson, Collection, Library of Congress.
Bottom: Photograph by Mathew B. Brady. Collection, Library of Congress.

24 Photograph. Collection, Library of Congress.

25 *Top:* Photograph. Collection, Library of Congress.
Bottom: Photograph by T. H. O'Sullivan, Collection, Library of Congress.

26 *Top:* Photograph. Cook Collection, Valentine Museum, Richmond, Va.
Bottom: Photograph by Mathew B. Brady. Collection, Library of Congress.

27-29 Collection, Music Division, Library of Congress.

30 Photograph. Brady-Handy Collection, Library of Congress.

31 Collection, Mr. John R. Peacock, High Point, North Carolina.

32 *Top:* Painting. Collection, Confederate Museum, Richmond, Va.
Bottom: Photograph by George N. Barnard. Collection, National Archives.

33 Photograph by Shipp or Gard, Lexington, Kentucky, October 1862. Collection, Mr. William H. Townsend.

34 *Left:* Photograph. Brady-Handy Collection, Library of Congress.
Right: Photograph. Collection, Library of Congress.

35 *Top:* Photograph by Mathew B. Brady. Collection, Library of Congress.
Bottom: Photograph. Collection, National Archives.

36 Photograph by Theodore Lilienthal, New Orleans, La. Collection, Library of Congress.

37 *Top:* Photograph. Collection, Library of Congress.
Bottom: Photograph. Collection, Library of Congress.

38 Photograph. Collection, Library of Congress.

39 Photograph. Collection, Library of Congress.

40 Photograph. Cook Collection, Valentine Museum, Richmond, Va.

41 Collection, Mr. John L. Rawls, Vienna, Va.

42 Map by James R. Johnson.

43 *Top:* Photograph by George W. Minnes. Cook Collection, Valentine Museum, Richmond, Va.
Bottom: Drawing by Alfred R. Waud. Collection, Library of Congress.

44 Photograph by Whitehurst. Collection, Library of Congress.

45 Photograph. Collection, National Archives.

46 Photograph by Alexander Gardner. Collection, National Archives.

47 Drawing by Frank H. Schell, 1862. Collection, New York-Historical Society, New York, N.Y.

48 *Top:* Photograph. Brady-Handy Collection, Library of Congress.
Bottom: Drawing by James R. Chapin. Collection, Library of Congress.

49 Drawing by Theodore R. Davis. Collection, Library of Congress.

50 Map by James R. Johnson.

51 Photograph. Collection, Library of Congress.

52 *Top:* Drawing by Alfred R. Waud. Collection, Library of Congress.
Bottom: Photograph by James F. Gibson. Collection, Library of Congress.

53 *Top:* Photograph. Collection, Library of Congress.
Bottom: Photograph. Collection, Library of Congress.

54 Photograph (retouched). Collection, Library of Congress.

55 Collection, The Handley Library, Winchester, Va.

56 *Left:* Photograph. Collection, Library of Congress.
Right: Ambrotype: Logan Collection, Illinois State Historical Library, Springfield.

57 Photograph by Capt. Andrew J. Russell. Collection, Library of Congress.

58 Photograph by T. H. O'Sullivan. Collection, Library of Congress.

59 *Top:* Photograph by Mathew B. Brady. Brady-Handy Collection, Library of Congress.
Bottom: Photograph by T. H. O'Sullivan. Collection, Library of Congress.

60 Photograph by Alexander, Fairfax Courthouse, Va. Collection, Mr. E. B. White, Leesburg, Va.

61 Photograph, 1865. Brady-Handy Collection, Library of Congress.

62 *Top:* Map by James R. Johnson.
Bottom: Photograph. Standing, left to right: Ben Palmer and Walter Gosden. Seated, left to right: Capt. W. R. Smith, Capt. R. P. Montjoy, Baron Von Massow. Cook Collection, Valentine Museum, Richmond, Va.

63 Wood-engraving. *Harper's Weekly,* 1863. Collection, Library of Congress.

64 Photograph by T. H. O'Sullivan. Collection, National Archives.

65 *Top:* Photograph by Mathew B. Brady. Collection, Library of Congress.
Bottom: Wood-engraving. *Frank Leslie's Illustrated Newspaper,* 1863. Collection, Library of Congress.

66 Photograph by Mathew B. Brady. Collection, National Archives.

67 Drawing by Alfred R. Waud. Collection, Library of Congress.

68 *Top:* Photograph. Cook Collection, Valentine Museum, Richmond, Va.
Bottom: Photograph by Mathew B. Brady. Brady-Handy Collection, Library of Congress.

69 *Top, left:* Photograph by Mathew B. Brady. Collection, Library of Congress.
Top, right: Photograph. Collection, Miss Alice Lee Parker, Washington, D.C.
Bottom: Drawing by Alfred R. Waud. Collection, Library of Congress.

70 *Top:* Photograph. Collection, Library of Congress.
Bottom: Drawing by Alfred R. Waud. Collection, Library of Congress.

71 *Top:* Photograph. Collection, National Archives.
Bottom: Collection, Music Division, Library of Congress.

72 Photograph by Mathew B. Brady. Collection, Library of Congress.

73 Drawing by Edwin Forbes. Collection, Library of Congress.

74 Photograph by T. H. O'Sullivan. Collection, Library of Congress.

75 Photograph by T. H. O'Sullivan. Collection, Library of Congress.

76 Map by James R. Johnson.

77 Photograph. Collection, Library of Congress.

78 Photograph by Mathew B. Brady. Collection, Library of Congress.

79 Photograph. Collection, Library of Congress.

80 Photograph. Collection, Library of Congress.

81 *Top:* Photograph. Cook Collection, Valentine Museum, Richmond, Va.
Bottom: Photograph by Mathew B. Brady. Collection, Library of Congress.

82 Photograph. Collection, Library of Congress.

83 Drawing by Alfred R. Waud. Collection, Library of Congress.

84 Map by James R. Johnson.

85 Photograph. Collection, Library of Congress.

86 Map by James R. Johnson.

87 *Top:* Wood-engraving. *Harper's Weekly,* 1863. Collection, Library of Congress.
Bottom: Photograph (retouched). Collection, Library of Congress.

88 *Top:* Photograph by T. H. O'Sullivan. Collection, Library of Congress.
Bottom: Photograph by T. H. O'Sullivan. Collection, Library of Congress.

89 *Top:* Tintype. Collection, Library of Congress.
Bottom: Photograph. Collection, Library of Congress.

90–91 *Top:* Drawing by Edwin Forbes. Collection, Library of Congress.

90 *Bottom:* Photograph. Collection, Library of Congress.

91 *Bottom:* Photograph. Collection, Library of Congress.

92 Drawing by Alfred R. Waud. Collection, Library of Congress.

93 *Top:* Photograph by T. H. O'Sullivan. Collection, Library of Congress.
Bottom: Wood-engraving. *Frank Leslie's Illustrated Newspaper,* 1863. Collection, Library of Congress.

94 Photograph by Mathew B. Brady. Brady-Handy Collection, Library of Congress.

95 Collection, Confederate Museum, Richmond, Va.

96 Map by James R. Johnson.

97 *Top:* Photograph by Mathew B. Brady. Brady-Handy Collection, Library of Congress.
Bottom: Wood-engraving. *Harper's Weekly,* 1862. Collection, Library of Congress.

98 *Top, left:* Photograph by Mathew B. Brady. Collection, Library of Congress.
Top, right: Photograph by Mathew B. Brady. Brady-Handy Collection, Library of Congress.
Bottom: Photograph by Alexander Gardner. Collection, Library of Congress.

99 *Top:* Broadside. Collection, Rare Book Room, Library of Congress.
Bottom: Photograph. Collection, Mrs. Katharine McCook Knox, Washington, D.C.

100 Photograph. Collection, Library of Congress.

101 Photograph. Collection, Library of Congress.

102 *Top:* Left, center and right. Photographs. Collection, Confederate Museum, Richmond, Va.
Bottom: Tintype. Collection, Library of Congress.

103 *Left:* Photograph by Mathew B. Brady. Collection, Library of Congress.
Right: Photograph (retouched). Collection, Kansas State Historical Society, Topeka.

104 Map by James R. Johnson.

105 *Top:* Photograph. Collection, Library of Congress.
Bottom: Drawing by Sherman Enderton, Co. E, 11th Kansas. Collection, Kansas State Historical Society, Topeka.

106 *Top, left:* Photograph. Collection, Mr. Carl Breihan, St. Louis, Mo.
Top, right: Photograph by Mathew B. Brady. Collection, Library of Congress.
Bottom: Engraving by John Sartain after painting by George Caleb Bingham. Collection, Library of Congress.

107 Drawing by A. S. Leclerc. Collection, Library of Congress.

108 Photograph. Collection, National Archives.

109 Collection, Mr. John L. Rawls, Vienna, Va.

110 Map by James R. Johnson.

111 *Top:* Photograph by Mathew B. Brady. Brady-Handy Collection, Library of Congress.
Bottom: Drawing by J. F. E. Hillen. Collection, New York Public Library, New York, N.Y.

112 *Top:* Photograph. Collection, Library of Congress.
Bottom: Photograph by Mathew B. Brady. Collection, Library of Congress.

113 Photograph. Collection, Library of Congress.

114 *Left:* Photograph by Mathew B. Brady. Collection, National Archives.
Right: Ambrotype: Collection, Texas History Center, University of Texas, Austin.

115 Painting by Carl Iwonski, *c.* 1862. Collection, Witte Memorial Museum, San Antonio, Texas.

116 *Top:* Photograph. Collection, Library of Congress.
Bottom: Drawing by J. F. E. Hillen. Collection, New York Public Library, New York, N.Y.

117 *Top:* Photograph by George N. Barnard. Collection, National Archives.
Bottom: Photograph. Collection, National Archives.

118 Photograph by T. H. O'Sullivan. Collection, Library of Congress.

119 Wood-engraving.

120 Photograph. Collection, Library of Congress.

121 Photograph by Mathew B. Brady. Collection, National Archives.

122 Photograph by T. H. O'Sullivan. Collection, Library of Congress.

123 *Top:* Drawing by Edwin Forbes. Collection, Library of Congress.
Bottom: Photograph by T. H. O'Sullivan. Collection, Library of Congress.

124 *Top:* Photograph. Collection, National Archives.
Bottom: Photograph. Brady-Handy Collection, Library of Congress.

125 Photograph by T. H. O'Sullivan. Collection, Library of Congress.

126 Photograph. Collection, Library of Congress.

127 Photograph. Collection, Library of Congress.

128 *Left:* Photograph by Mathew B. Brady. Brady-Handy Collection, Library of Congress.
Right: Drawing by Alfred R. Waud. Collection, Library of Congress.

129 *Top:* Drawing by Alfred R. Waud. Collection, Library of Congress.
Bottom: Photograph by Mathew B. Brady. Brady-Handy Collection, Library of Congress.

130 *Top:* Ambrotype. Collection, Chicago Historical Society, Chicago, Ill.
Bottom: Drawing by Alfred R. Waud. Collection, Library of Congress.

131 *Top.* Photograph. Collection, Library of Congress.
Bottom: Drawing by Alfred R. Waud. Collection, Library of Congress.

132 Photograph by Mathew B. Brady. Brady-Handy Collection, Library of Congress.

133 Drawing by Alfred R. Waud. Collection, Library of Congress.

134 Drawing by Arthur Lumley. Collection, Library of Congress.

135 *Top:* Photograph. Collection, National Archives.
Bottom: Photograph. Collection, Library of Congress.

136 Map by James R. Johnson.

137 Photograph. Cook Collection. Valentine Museum, Richmond, Va.

138 Photograph. Collection, Library of Congress.

139 *Top:* Photograph. Collection, Library of Congress.
Bottom: Drawing by Alfred R. Waud. Collection, Library of Congress.

140 *Top:* Photograph. Collection, Library of Congress.
Bottom, left: Photograph by Mathew B. Brady, Collection, Library of Congress.
Bottom, right: Photograph. Cook Collection, Valentine Museum, Richmond, Va.

141 Photograph by Mathew B. Brady. Collection, Library of Congress.

142 Photograph by Alexander Gardner. Collection, Library of Congress.

143 *Top:* Drawing by Alfred R. Waud. Collection, Library of Congress.
Bottom: Photograph by T. H. O'Sullivan. Collection, Library of Congress.

144 Photograph by T. H. O'Sullivan. Collection, Library of Congress.

145 Photograph by T. H. O'Sullivan. Collection, Library of Congress.

146 Photograph. Collection, National Archives.

147 Drawing. Collection, New York Public Library, New York, N.Y.

148 Photograph by Mathew B. Brady. Collection, National Archives.

149 Drawing by Arthur Lumley. Collection, New York Public Library, New York, N.Y.

150 *Top:* Ambrotype. Collection, Confederate Museum, Richmond, Va.
   Bottom: Photograph. Collection, Library of Congress.

151 *Top:* Photograph by Mathew B. Brady. Collection, Library of Congress.
   Bottom: Photograph. Collection, Library of Congress.

152 Photograph. Collection, Library of Congress.

153 *Left:* Photograph by Mathew B. Brady. Collection, Library of Congress.
   Right: Photograph by Mathew B. Brady. Collection, Library of Congress.

154 *Top:* Photograph by Mathew B. Brady. Collection, Library of Congress.
   Bottom: Ambrotype. Collection, Confederate Museum, Richmond, Va.

155 Drawing by Edwin Forbes. Collection, Library of Congress.

156 Photograph. Collection, National Archives.

157 Drawing by Louis Maurer. Collection, New York Public Library, New York, N.Y.

158 *Top:* Map by James R. Johnson.
   Bottom: Photograph. Cook Collection, Valentine Museum, Richmond, Va.

159 *Top:* Photograph. Collection, Library of Congress.
   Bottom: Drawing by Alfred R. Waud. Collection, Library of Congress.

160 Drawing by Alfred R. Waud. Collection, Library of Congress.

161 Photograph. Collection, National Archives.

162 Drawing by Alfred R. Waud. Collection, Library of Congress.

163 *Top:* Photograph by Mathew B. Brady. Collection Library of Congress.
   Bottom: Photograph. Collection, National Archives.

164 Photograph by T. H. O'Sullivan. Collection, Library of Congress.

165 Photograph. Collection, Library of Congress.

166 Photograph. Cook Collection, Valentine Museum, Richmond, Va.

167 Drawing by Alfred R. Waud. Collection, Library of Congress.

168 Photograph by Charles E. Meyer. Collection, Library of Congress.

169 *Top:* Photograph. Collection, Mr. Ezra J. Warner, La Jolla, Cal.
   Bottom: Photograph by Charles E. Meyer. Collection, Library of Congress.

170 *Top:* Photograph. Brady-Handy Collection, Library of Congress.
   Bottom: Photograph. Collection, National Archives.

171 *Top:* Photograph by Mathew B. Brady. Collection, Library of Congress.
   Bottom: Photograph by Mathew B. Brady. Brady-Handy Collection, Library of Congress.

172 Drawing by Alfred R. Waud. Collection, Library of Congress.

173 *Top:* Photograph. Collection, National Archives.
   Bottom: Photograph by T. H. O'Sullivan. Collection, Library of Congress.

174 Drawing by Alfred R. Waud. Collection, Library of Congress.

175 Drawing by Alfred R. Waud. Collection, Library of Congress.

176 *Top:* Photograph. Brady-Handy Collection, Library of Congress.
   Bottom: Photograph by T. H. O'Sullivan. Collection, Library of Congress.

177 Drawing by Alfred R. Waud. Collection, Library of Congress.

178 Photograph by Mathew B. Brady. Collection, Library of Congress.

179 *Top:* Music cover. Collection, Music Division, Library of Congress.
   Bottom: Drawing by Arthur Lumley. Collection, Library of Congress.

180–183 Collection, Music Division, Library of Congress.

184 Photograph. Cook Collection, Valentine Museum, Richmond, Va.

185 Collection, Miss Frances McCook and Mr. Anson T. McCook, Hartford, Conn.

186 Photograph. Collection, Library of Congress.

187 Map by James R. Johnson.

188–89 Drawing by Alfred R. Waud. Collection, Library of Congress.

190 Photograph by Mathew B. Brady. Collection, Library of Congress.

191 *Top:* Photograph by Mathew B. Brady. Collection, Library of Congress.
   Bottom: Photograph. Collection, Library of Congress.

192 Photograph. Collection, National Archives.

193 *Top:* Photograph. Collection, Library of Congress.
   Bottom: Tintype. Collection, Miss Josephine Cobb, Arlington, Va.

194 Photograph by John A. Scholten. Collection, Library of Congress.

195 Collection, Mr. John L. Rawls, Vienna, Va.

196 *Top:* Photograph. Collection, Library of Congress.
Bottom: Photograph (retouched). Collection, Library of Congress.

197 Photograph by Mathew B. Brady. Collection, National Archives.

198 *Top:* Photograph. Collection, Library of Congress.
Bottom: Photograph by George N. Barnard. Collection, Library of Congress.

199 *Top:* Photograph by Mathew B. Brady. Brady-Handy Collection, Library of Congress.
Bottom: Photograph. Collection, National Archives.

200 Photograph. Collection, Library of Congress.

201 Photograph by George N. Barnard. Collection, Library of Congress.

202 Photograph by George N. Barnard. Collection, Library of Congress.

203 Photograph by George N. Barnard. Collection, Library of Congress.

204 *Top:* Photograph. Collection, Library of Congress.
Bottom: Tintype. Collection, Missouri Historical Society, St. Louis, Mo.

205 Photograph by George N. Barnard. Collection, Library of Congress.

206 Photograph. Collection, National Archives.

207 Collection, West Point Museum, U. S. Military Academy, West Point, N.Y.

208 Photograph by T. H. O'Sullivan. Collection, Library of Congress.

209 *Top:* Photograph. Southern Historical Collection, University of North Carolina, Chapel Hill, N.C.
Bottom: Drawing by Alfred R. Waud. Collection, Library of Congress.

210 Photograph. Collection, Library of Congress.

211 Photograph. Collection, Library of Congress.

213 Drawing by Alfred R. Waud. Collection, Library of Congress.

214 Photograph by A. J. Riddle. Collection, Library of Congress.

215 Photograph by Mathew B. Brady. Collection, Library of Congress.

Alabama, 83, 84, 196, 200, 202, 214
Albemarle County, Va., 127
Albuquerque, N. M., 37
Aldie, Va., 67
Alexandria, Va., 45, 48, 70
Alston, Capt. R. A., CSA, 99
Amelia Court House, Va., 212
Ames, Sgt., USA and CSA, 66
Ames, 6
Anderson's Crossroads, Tenn., 110
Antietam Creek, Md., 46, 49
Apache Canyon, N. M., 38
Appalachians, 31
Appomattox, Va., 212, 213
Appomattox River, Va., 164
Arkansas, 34
Arlington, Va., 9
Ash, Capt., USA, 130
Ashby, Col. Henry M., CSA, 116
Ashby, Capt. Turner, CSA, 6, 7, 8
Ashby Gap, Va., 90
Ashland, Va., 77, 124
Athens, Ala., 196
Athens, Ga., 215
Atlanta, Ga., 83, 165, 195, 201, 203
Attila, 175
Auburn, Va., 88
Averell, Gen. W. W., USA, 26, 67, 74, 75, 171, 175

Banks, Gen. N. P., USA, 8, 41
Banks Ford, Va., 71, 131
Barteau, Col. C. R., CSA, 86
Batesville, Ark., 34
Baton Rouge, La., 86, 87
Beale, Gen. R. L. T., CSA, 126
Beauregard, Gen. P. G. T., CSA, 8, 9, 33, 158, 205, 212
Beaver Dam Station, Va., 123, 137
Belle Isle, Va., 120, 126
Belle Plain, Va., 133, 135
Bentonville, N. C., 210
Bermuda Hundred, Va., 140
Birmingham, Ala., 205
Blackford, Capt. Charles M., CSA, 6
Blackford, Capt. W. W., CSA, 13, 26, 51, 52, 88
Blackwater Creek, Va., 158, 162, 187, 190
Blair, Montgomery, 168
Blue Ridge Mountains, Va., 90, 174
Blunt, Gen. James G., USA, 107
Boker, Henry, 6
Boonsboro, Md., 93
Booth, John Wilkes, 68
Borcke, Heros von, CSA, 26
Bottom's Bridge, Va., 127

Bowling Green, Va., 80
Bragg, Gen. Braxton, CSA, 55, 56, 57, 83, 84, 86, 95, 109, 117, 141, 195
Brandy Station, Va., 74, 75, 88, 92, 135
Brian, Col. L. T., CSA, 44
Brice's Crossroads, Miss., 195
Bristoe, Va., 119
Bristoe Station, Va., 45, 173
Broadhead, Col. T. F., USA, 12
Broad Run, Va., 119
Brockman, Sgt. Lewis F., USA, 8
Brown, John, 7, 103
Brownlow, William G., 98, 101
Buckland Mills, Va., 119
Buckner, Gen. Simon B., CSA, 102
Buena Vista, Mexico, 3, 26
Buffington Island, Ohio, 99, 100
Buford, Gen. John, USA, 3, 80, 81, 93
Buford, Gen. N. P., USA, 67, 74
Bull Run, Va., 9, 66
Bunker Hill, Va., 178
Burke, Redmond, CSA, 21
Burke's Station, Va., 58, 212
Burkesville, Ky., 95
Burkeville, Va., 157, 159, 160, 211
Burnside, Gen. Ambrose, USA, 57, 67, 97, 100
Burton's Ford, Va., 131
Butler, Gen. B. F., USA, 134, 140, 141, 142, 158
Butler, Gen. Matthew C., CSA, 48, 51
Butler, Mo., 104

Cameron, Simon, Secretary of War, 4
Camp Douglas, Chicago, 97
Canby, Gen. Edward R. S., USA, 36, 37, 39
Capehart, Lt. Col. Charles E., USA, 11
Carlisle, Pa., 51, 52
Carper, Pvt. Phillip W., CSA, 14
Carr's Bridge, Va., 76
Carthage, Mo., 34
Castle Murray, Va., 88
Catlett's Station, Va., 42, 43, 45, 59, 67
Catockin Creek, Md., 47
Cedar Creek, Va., 43, 44, 67, 177
Cedar Mountain, Va., 41
Centerville, Va., 65, 66
Chalmers, Gen. J. R., CSA, 196, 199, 200
Chambersburg, Pa., 48, 51, 168, 169, 170
Chambliss, Col. J. R., CSA, 57, 153, 203
Chantilly, Va., 65
Chancellorsville, Va., 71, 81, 88, 92, 129
Chapman, Col. George H., USA, 137, 138
Charles City Court House, Va., 153, 155
Chattanooga, Tenn., 37, 59, 83, 109, 110, 115, 116, 117, 198

Charlottesville, Va., 55, 122, 127, 129, 149, 151
Chesnut, Gen. James, CSA, 78
Chesnut, Mrs. Mary B., 78, 185
Chesterfield Bridge, Va., 145
Chew, Capt., CSA, 131
Chicago, Ill., 97
Chickahominy River, Va., 17, 18, 24, 25, 78, 124, 141, 153
Chickamauga, Ga., 109
Childs, Col. James E., USA, 12
Childsburg, Va., 137
Cincinnati, Ohio, 99, 101
City Point, Va., 186
Cluke, Col. Roy S., CSA, 99
Coggins Point, Va., 186, 188
Coke, Col. Richard, CSA, 3
Cold Harbor, Va., 144, 147
Cole, Sgt. Daniel R., USA, 53
Columbia, Ky., 95
Columbia, Mo., 41
Columbia, S. C., 205
Columbia, Tenn., 55
Columbia, Va., 79
Conococheague River, 51
Coogle, Adam, 47
Cooke, Gen. Phillip St. George, USA, 22, 23, 73
Cook's Mill, Va., 187
Corbett, Sgt. "Boston," USA, 68
Corinth, Miss., 83, 201
Cottonport, Tenn., 110
Corydon, Ind., 99
Couch, Gen. D. N., USA, 170
Covode, Col. G. H., USA, 154, 155
Crook, Gen. George, USA, 111, 168
Croxton, Gen. John, USA, 205
Cub Run, Va., 66
Culpeper, Va., 67, 92, 119, 122, 127
Culpeper Court House, Va., 74
Cumberland Landing, Va., 19
Cumberland River, 32, 35, 55, 83, 95
Curtin, Andrew G., 171
Custer, Gen. George A., USA, 93, 119, 127, 128, 129, 130,
    131, 137, 138, 139, 142, 144, 147, 150, 176, 177, 178,
    179, 213

Dahlgren, Adm. John, USN, 123
Dahlgren, Col. Uric, USA, 123, 124, 125, 126, 127
Danville, Va., 212
Davenport Bridge, Va., 137
Davis, Col. Hasbrock, USA, 77, 78
Davis, Jefferson, 4, 26, 49, 78, 109, 126, 127, 141, 195, 196,
    197, 210, 211, 212, 213, 214, 215
Davis, Mrs. Jefferson, 78, 202, 210, 214
Davies, Gen. H. E., USA, 170, 190, 209
Dearing, Gen., CSA, 187
Decatur, Miss., 86
Deep Bottom, Va., 153
DeForest, William, USA, 172
Deitzler, Gen. George, USA, 105
Dennison, Capt., USA, 154
Devins, Gen., USA, 137
Dinwiddie Court House, Va., 159, 211
Dodge, Gen. Grenville, USA, 83, 84
Don Bazan, 14
Dover Mills, Va., 125
Duck River, Tenn., 112
Duffie, Col. A. N., USA, 178, 179
Duke, Gen. Basil, CSA, 102

Durham's Station, N. C., 212

Early, Gen. Jubal A., CSA, 166, 167, 168, 169, 171, 172, 175,
    211
Eastport, Miss., 83
Elizabethtown, Ky., 56
Ellett, Gen. Alfred W., USA, 35, 83
Elyton, Ala., 205
Emmitsburg, Md., 52
Emory, Gen. W. H., USA, 22
Etowah River, Ga., 83
Ewing, Gen. Thomas, USA, 104, 106, 107

Fairfax, Va., 9, 64, 66
Fairfax Court House, Va., 8, 63, 64, 66
Fairfax County, Va., 64
Falling Water Bridge, Tenn., 117
Falmouth, Va., 67
Farmington, Tenn., 114
Fauquier County, Va., 64
Fayetteville, N. C., 205
Ferris, Pvt. Achille, CSA, 114
Fisher's Hill, Va., 175
Five Forks, Va., 211
Fleetwood Heights, Va., 88
Flint, Capt. Edward A., USA, 93
Florida, 214
Ford's Station, Va., 158, 159
Forrest, Gen. N. B., CSA, 3, 30, 31, 32, 33, 39, 55, 83, 84, 85,
    109, 110, 195, 196, 199, 200, 201, 202, 205
Fort Bliss, Texas, 37
Fort Craig, N. M., 37
Fort Delaware, 215
Fort Donelson, Tenn., 32
Fort Fisher, N. C., 207
Fort Henry, Tenn., 32
Fort Marcy, N. M., 37, 38
Fort Monroe, Va., 142
Fort Powhatan, Va., 187
Fort Scott, Kan., 107
Fort Stedman, Va., 208, 211
Fort Stevens, D. C., 167
Franklin, Tenn., 202
Fredericks Hall Station, Va., 124
Fredericksburg, Va., 57, 71, 134, 151
Fredericktown, Md., 92, 167
Freeman's Ford, Va., 42
Frémont, Gen. J. C., USA, 41
Front Royal, Va., 178

Gainesville, Ala., 205
Gainesville, Va., 44
Garfield, Gen. James, USA, 83
Garlick's Landing, Va., 19, 20, 21, 23
George, Pvt. Alexander Spiers, CSA, 14
Georgetown, Ohio, 158
Georgia, 26, 83, 84, 90, 157, 195, 214
Germanna Ford, Va., 73, 74, 75
Gettysburg, Pa., 80, 91, 92, 93, 95, 119
Gibbs, Col. Alfred, USA, 137
Giesboro, Md., 89
Gillem, Gen. A. C., USA, 203, 204
Gilmor, Col. Harry, CSA, 168, 169, 170
Glasgow, Ky., 56
Glorietta Pass, N. M., 37
Gloucester Point, Va., 78, 79
Goochland, Va., 123

232

Gooding, Billy, 70
Gordon, Gen. James B., CSA, 140, 141
Gordonsville, Va., 76, 80, 149, 151, 210
Graffam, Sgt. Joshua P., USA, 193
Granger, Gen. Gordon, USA, 112
Grant, Gen. U. S., USA, 32, 33, 39, 56, 85, 86, 115, 117, 133,
    134, 144, 145, 147, 148, 153, 165, 168, 172, 175, 186,
    192, 193, 199, 208, 209, 211, 212
Greeley, Horace, 79
Green, Col. John Shac, CSA, 139
Green Springs Valley, Va., 149
Greenville, Tenn., 203
Gregg, Gen. David M., USA, 74, 76, 77, 79, 134, 144, 147,
    149, 153, 154, 155, 170
Green River Bridge, Ky., 95
Greensboro, N. C., 212, 213, 214
Grierson, Col. Benjamin, USA, 85, 86, 87, 195
Guild, George, CSA, 114

Hagerstown, Md., 51, 92, 167
Halleck, Gen. H. W., USA, 34, 39, 104, 120, 170
Hanson, Col. C. S., USA, 96
Hampton, Gen. Wade, CSA, 3, 51, 80, 149, 150, 152, 153,
    154, 157, 161, 184, 185, 186, 188, 189, 190, 193, 203, 204,
    205, 212, 213, 214
Hancock, Md., 171
Hanover Court House, Va., 18, 126
Hanover Creek, Va., 144
Hanover Junction, Pa., 91, 92, 149
Hanover Station, Va., 77, 144, 147
Hanson, Roger W., USA, 195
Harlan, Col. John M., USA, 55, 56
Harpers Ferry, Va., 49, 59, 103
Harris, Governor of Tenn., 31
Harrison's Landing, Va., 26
Hartsville, Ky., 55
Hatch, Col. Edward, USA, 86
Hawe's (Haw's) Machine Shop, Va., 18, 147
Hays, Capt. Henry B., USA, 11
Heintzelman, Gen. S. P., USA, 58, 59, 66
Helena, Ark., 34
Higgins, Col. Jacob, USA, 11
High Bridge, Va., 157, 159, 160
Hildebrand, Samuel, CSA, 106
Hill, Gen. A. P., CSA, 47
Hines, Capt. Thomas H., CSA, 97
Hoke, Gen. R. F., CSA, 158
Holly Springs, Miss., 56
Holston River, Tenn., 101
Hood, Gen. J. B., CSA, 195, 202, 207
Hooker, Gen. Joseph "Fighting Joe," USA, 67, 71, 73, 75,
    79, 81, 88, 92, 115, 116
Hoskins, Capt. B. S., CSA, 68
Humboldt, Tenn., 56
Hungary Station, Va., 78, 126
Hunter, Gen. David, USA, 148, 149, 151, 167, 168
Hurt, Sgt. D. M., USA, 56

Illinois, 102
Imboden, Gen. John D., CSA, 173
Independence, Mo., 107
Indiana, 96, 97, 99, 102, 103, 199
Indianapolis, Ind., 99
Ingalls, Col. Rufus, USA, 21, 23
Ingersoll, Col. R. G., USA, 55
Island No. Ten, 41

Jackson, Andrew, 185
Jackson, Tenn., 56
Jackson, Gen. Thomas J. "Stonewall," CSA, 8, 9, 17, 25,
    28, 41, 43, 44, 45, 46, 47, 48, 49, 81, 167, 199
Jacksonport Ark., 34
James, Frank, CSA, 105
James, Jesse, 107
James River, Va., 25, 26, 79, 120, 123, 125, 126, 134, 140,
    147, 149, 151, 152, 153, 155, 162, 168, 207
Jasper, Tenn., 111
Jefferson, Thomas, 212
Jeffersonton, Va., 209
Jennison, Charles, 104
Jetersville, Va., 209
Johnson, Gen. Adam R., CSA, 100
Johnson, Gen. Bradley, CSA, 170, 171
Johnson, CSA, 211
Johnsonville, Tenn., 199, 200, 201
Johnston, Gen. A. S., CSA, 33
Johnston, Gen. Joseph, CSA, 5, 8, 9, 15, 195, 206, 210, 211,
    212, 213
Johnstone, Col. Robert, USA, 66
Jones, Col. "Grumble," CSA, 52
Jones's Landing, Va., 152
Judah, Gen. Henry M., USA, 98
Jude's Ferry, Va., 125

Kanawha Canal, Va., 125
Kansas, 103, 105
Kautz, Gen. A. V., USA, 157, 158, 159, 160, 161, 162, 187,
    189, 190
Kelly's Ford, Va., 58, 67, 73, 75, 178
Kentucky, 31, 32, 33, 34, 55, 56, 95, 107, 203
Kilpatrick, Gen. Judson, USA, 3, 78, 118, 119, 120, 122, 123,
    124, 125, 126, 127, 131, 201, 203, 205, 215
King and Queen Court House, Va., 126
Knoxville, Md., 51
Knoxville, Tenn., 100, 101, 102

LaGrange, Tenn., 86
Lane, James H., 103, 104, 105
Lane, Col. Walter P., CSA, 34
Latane, Capt. William, CSA, 18, 25
Lawrence, Kan., 104, 106
Lebanon, Ky., 96, 99
Lee, Col. Custis, CSA, 78, 124, 131
Lee, Col. Fitzhugh, CSA, 17, 18, 19, 66, 67, 75, 119, 129, 137,
    147, 149, 151, 154, 208, 211
Lee, Gen. Robert E., CSA, 14, 15, 17, 18, 23, 25, 41, 42, 44,
    49, 51, 71, 79, 80, 81, 91, 92, 93, 99, 101, 119, 120, 124,
    127, 133, 134, 137, 142, 145, 147, 157, 158, 159, 167,
    172, 185, 186, 187, 207, 209, 210, 211, 212, 213
Lee, Col. W. H. F., "Rooney," CSA, 17, 21, 23, 24, 75, 80,
    81, 159, 161, 162, 185, 190
Leesburg, Va., 168
Leib, Lt. E. H., USA, 18
Lexington, Mo., 34
Lexington, Tenn., 55
Lexington, Va., 151
Libby Prison, Richmond, 98, 100
Lighthouse Point, Va., 163
Lincoln, Abraham, 4, 26, 39, 41, 52, 67, 68, 71, 104, 120, 121
    122, 167, 213
Little River, Va., 147
Lomax, Gen. L. L., CSA, 139, 151, 176, 177
Lookout Mountain, Tenn., 90

Loring, Gen., CSA, 86
Loudoun County, Va., 59, 64, 175, 179
Louisa Court House, Va., 76, 149
Louisiana, 95, 196
Louisville, Ky., 56, 95, 107
Lunenburg County, Va., 162
Luray Valley, Va., 175
Lyman, Col. Theodore, USA, 122, 127, 133, 171
Lynchburg, Va., 129, 160, 212

McCabe, Lt. Col. George, USA, 2
McCausland, Gen. John, CSA, 168, 169, 170, 171
McClellan, Gen. George B., USA, 14, 17, 19, 25, 26, 49, 51,
    52, 57, 73
McConnellsburg, Md., 171
McCook, Maj. Daniel, USA, 99
McCook, Gen. Edward Moody, USA, 185
McCoy's Ford, 49, 51
McCord, Mrs. 202
McCreary, J. B., CSA, 99, 100
McDowell, Gen. Irvin, USA, 41, 44, 119
McIntosh, Col. J. B., USA, 93, 140, 141
McMahon, Gen. M. T., USA, 127
McMinnville, Tenn., 112
Macon, Ga., 214
Madison Court House, Va., 127, 128, 131
Mallory's Cross Roads, Va., 157
Malvern Hill, Va., 26
Manakin's Ferry, Va., 125
Manassas, Va., 7, 8, 9, 18, 33, 45, 46, 48, 57, 66, 119, 185
Manchester, Va., 211
Mann, Col. W. D., USA, 68, 69
Maps: Grierson's Raid, 86
        Hampton's Cattle Raid, 187
        Morgan's Indiana and Ohio Raid, 96
        Quantrill's Lawrence Raid, 76
        Sheridan's Raids, 136
        Stoneman's Raid, 76
        Streight's Raid, 84
        Stuart's Chambersburg Raid, 50
        Stuart's Chickahominy Ride, 22
        Stuart's Raid on Catlett's Station, 42
        Wheeler's Tennessee Raid, 110
        Wilson's Raid on Lee's Railroads, 158
Marmaduke, Gen. John S., CSA, 104, 105
Martin, Negro slave, 125
Martin, Col. W. T., CSA, 17, 20
Martinsburg, Va., 14, 167, 168
Mattapony River, Va., 145, 152
Maryland, 49, 59, 92, 174
Mason, Capt. J. W., USA, 71
May, Capt. C. A., USA, 3
Mayo's Bridge, Richmond, Va., 124, 126, 211
Mead, Capt. William Wormsley, CSA, 15
Meade, Pvt. David A., CSA, 150
Meade, Gen. George Gordon, USA, 119, 120, 122, 127, 128,
    129, 133, 134, 155, 158, 193
Meadow Bridge, Va., 78, 124, 141
Mechanicsville, Va., 124, 141
Meems, David, 125
Meigs, U. S. Quartermaster General, 58
Memphis, Tenn., 31, 195, 196, 199
Mercersburg, Md., 51
Merritt, Gen. Wesley, USA, 134, 137, 141, 142, 144, 145,
    170, 175
Mexico, 212
Milford, Va., 175

Milroy, Gen. R. H., USA, 199
Minger's Ferry, Va., 187
Mitchell, Gen. Ormsby, USA, 83
Mitchell, Gen. Robert, B., USA, 112, 115
Missionary Ridge, Tenn., 117
Mississippi, 33, 85, 86, 195, 196
Mississippi River, 41, 85
Missouri, 31, 34, 103, 104, 105, 106
Montevallo, Ala., 205
Montgomery, Ala., 109
Moore, Col. O. H., USA, 95
Moorefield, W. Va., 171
Moorman, Capt. M. N., CSA, 130
Morgan, Capt. C. H., CSA, 102
Morgan, Col. Dick, CSA, 102
Morgan, Gen. John Hunt, CSA, 3, 33, 34, 39, 54, 55, 56, 83,
    95, 96, 97, 98, 99, 100, 101, 102, 103, 104, 203
Morgan, Thomas, CSA, 95
Morgan's Lock, Va., 125
Morrison, Col. Andrew J., USA, 11
Morton, O. P., 97
Mount Crawford, Va., 172
Mount Jackson, Va., 177
Mosby, Col. John S., CSA, 60, 61, 62, 63, 64, 65, 66, 67, 68,
    70, 174, 175, 178, 179
Muldraugh's Hill, Ky., 56
Mumford, Col. Thomas T., CSA, 45
Munson, John, CSA, 64
Murfreesboro, Tenn., 55, 56, 57, 112
Murray, J. P., 41
Muscle Shoals, Ala., 114

Napoleon, Prince, 14
Nashville, Tenn., 32, 33, 83, 113, 195, 199, 201, 202, 207
Nast, Thomas, 97
Nevada, Mo., 104
New Kent, Va., 18
New Madrid, Mo., 41
New Mexico, 39
New York, 73, 127
Nichols, Gen. F. T., CSA, 129, 130
Nichols, Lt. Col. George S., USA, 153
North Anna River, Va., 76, 143, 144, 145, 147, 152
North Carolina, 157, 211, 212
Nottoway Court House, Va., 159
Nottoway River, Va., 162

Ohio, 96, 99, 102, 103, 199
Ohio River, 83, 97, 203
Old Church, Va., 18
Opequon, Va., 172, 175
Orloff, C., 7
Osceola, Mo., 104

Paine's Crossroads, Va., 209
Pamunkey River, Va., 19, 142, 143, 147, 152
Patterson, Gen. Robert, USA, 9
Pea Ridge, Ark., 34
Pearl River Bridge, Miss., 86
Peedee River, S. C., 204
Pelham, Maj. John, CSA, 57, 67, 68
Pemberton, Gen. J. C., CSA, 86
Peninsula, Va., 26, 44
Pennington, Lt. Alex. C. M., USA, 141
Pennsylvania, 29, 49, 92, 100, 101, 174
Pennsylvania Avenue, Washington, D. C., 4, 215

Petersburg, Va., 155, 157, 158, 159, 163, 185, 186, 191, 207, 208, 210, 211
Peuchelstein, Maj. A. von, 12
Philadelphia, Pa., 171
Pickett, Gen. George, CSA, 73, 211
Pillow, Gen. G. J., CSA, 33
Pittsburg Landing, Tenn., 33
Pleasonton, Gen. Alfred, USA, 51, 53, 81, 88, 91, 92, 120, 131, 133, 134
Pocahontas, Ark., 34
Point of Rocks, 8
Pony Mountain, Va., 128
Poolesville, Md., 59
Pope, Gen. John, USA, 41, 42, 43, 44, 45, 48, 49
Port Gibson, Miss., 87
Porter, Adm. David, USN, 85
Porter, Gen. Fitz John, USA, 18, 20, 22, 25
Potomac River, 7, 8, 17, 49, 51, 52, 167, 171
Powell, Pvt. Charles H., CSA, 18
Price, Gen. Sterling, CSA, 34, 104
Pulaski, Tenn., 199

Quantrill, Col. William C., CSA, 95, 103, 104, 105, 106, 107

Raccoon Ford, Va., 75, 81
Raccoon Mountain, Tenn., 116, 117
Randol, Capt. A. M., USA, 153, 154
Randolph, J. W., 27
Rapidan River, Va., 75, 119, 123, 131, 135
Rappahannock River, Va., 41, 42, 44, 48, 57, 67, 69, 79, 88
Rasin, Capt. William E., CSA, 15
Read, T. Buchanan, 180
Ream's Station, Va., 161
Rector's Crossroads, Va., 65
Resaca de la Palma, 3
Richmond, Va., 4, 14, 17, 25, 27, 74, 77, 78, 98, 109, 120, 122, 123, 124, 125, 126, 127, 129, 137, 138, 139, 141, 142, 145, 147, 155, 159, 160, 163, 165, 167, 185, 202, 203, 207, 210, 211, 212
Rio Grande River, 38
Ripley, Miss., 195
Rivanna River, Va., 127, 129, 131
Roanoke Bridge, Va., 157, 160
Roanoke River, Va., 157
Roanoke Station, Va., 160
Robertson, Capt. James M., USA, 79, 80
Robinson, Charles, 105
Rome, Ga., 83
Rosecrans, Gen. William S., USA, 57, 83, 95, 109, 112, 114, 116
Rosser, Gen. Thomas L., CSA, 40, 43, 44, 150, 187, 212
Rousseau, Gen. L. H., USA, 199
Rowanty Creek, Va., 186
Royall, Capt. W. B., CSA, 18, 23
Running Water Creek Gap, Tenn., 198
Rush, Col. Richard H., USA, 25

Sackett, Col. William, USA, 150, 151
Sand Mountain, Alabama, 83
Santa Fe, N. M., 38
Savannah, Ga., 203, 204, 207
Schofield, Gen. J. M., USA, 104, 107, 202
Scotsville, Va., 210
Scott, Dred, 168
Scott, Col. John S., CSA, 102
Scott, Gen. Winfield, 4, 39
Seddon, James A., 125

Sedgewick, Gen. John, USA, 127
Selma, Ala., 205
Semmes, Adm. Raphael, CSN, 210
Sequatchie Valley, Tenn., 110, 111
Shackleford, Gen. J. M., USA, 100
Shadburne, Sgt. George, CSA, 186
Shannon's Crossroads, Va., 80
Sharpsburg, Md., 46, 49
Shawneetown, Ill., 157
Shelby, Gen. Joseph, CSA, 32, 34, 35, 104
Shelbyville, Tenn., 112
Shenandoah Valley, Va., 5, 7, 8, 9, 17, 46, 57, 73, 149, 167, 168, 171, 172, 177, 179, 200
Shepherdstown, W. Va., 53
Sheridan, Gen. P. H., USA, 3, 39, 132, 134, 135, 137, 138, 141, 142, 143, 144, 145, 147, 148, 149, 152, 153, 154, 155, 157, 164, 167, 170, 171, 172, 174, 175, 177, 178, 179, 180, 181, 182, 183, 205, 207, 210, 211, 212, 213, 215
Sherman, Gen. W. T., USA, 5, 13, 33, 39, 157, 195, 196, 198, 199, 200, 201, 203, 205, 210, 212
Shiloh Church, Tenn., 33, 35, 109
Shuler, Pvt. Jonas Nathan, USA, 13
Sibley, Gen. Henry H., CSA, 37, 38
Sigel, Gen. Franz, USA, 167
Sixteen-Mile Turnout, Va., 160
Smith, Gen. Sooy, USA, 195
Snicker's Gap, Va., 179
South Anna River, Va., 17, 77, 79, 124, 125, 126, 137
South Carolina, 185, 203, 204, 205
Springfield, Mo., 34
Spotsylvania Court House, Va., 123, 134, 137, 145, 152
St. John's Church, Va., 162
St. Louis, Mo., 39
St. Mary's Church, Va., 153
St. Peter's Church, Va., 24, 25
Stanley, Gen. David S., USA, 114
Stanardsville, Va., 128, 131
Stanton, E. M., 170
Staunton River, Va., 160
Steele, Gen. Frederick, USA, 34, 35
Stevensburg, Va., 74
Stevenson, Ala., 115
Stoneman, Gen. George, USA, 71, 72, 73, 74, 75, 76, 79, 80, 81, 88, 120, 133, 205
Stones River, Tenn., 57, 112
Stony Brook Depot, Va., 161
Stoughton, Gen. Edwin H., USA, 66
Strasburg, Va., 171, 172
Streight, Col. Abel D., USA, 82, 83, 84, 85, 90, 98, 100
Stuart, Gen. J. E. B., CSA, 3, 5, 7, 8, 9, 13, 14, 15, 16, 17, 18, 21, 23, 24, 25, 26, 29, 41, 42, 43, 44, 46, 47, 49, 51, 52, 53, 55, 57, 58, 60, 63, 66, 67, 69, 73, 74, 75, 79, 88, 91, 92, 93, 95, 119, 130, 131, 134, 137, 138, 142, 185, 203, 209
Stuart, J. E. B., Jr., 67
Sturgis, Gen. Samuel D., USA, 194, 195
"Suck, The" (Tennessee River), 116, 117
Sudley Road, Va., 13
Sudley Springs Ford, Va., 66
Swain, Col. James B., USA, 12
"Sweeney," J. E. B. Stuart's troubadour, 58
Sycamore Church, Va., 186, 187, 190

Ta River, Va., 137
Tappan, Lt. Col. Samuel F., USA, 39
Taylor, Gen. Richard, CSA, 196
Taylor, Gen. Zachary, USA, 3

235

Tennessee, 33, 34, 35, 39, 56, 83, 85, 95, 109, 195, 200, 205, 212
Tennessee River, 32, 33, 109, 110, 114, 115, 116, 196, 200
Texas, 212, 213
Thomas, Gen. G. H., USA, 202
Thomason, Col. John, USMC, 75, 139
Thompson, Capt. James A., CSA, 3
Tipton, Mo., 107
Torbert, Gen. A. T. A., USA, 146, 147, 149, 151, 153, 170, 175
Totopotomy Creek, Va., 18
Trenton, Tenn., 56
Trevilian Station, Va., 149, 151, 152
Trimble, Gen. Isaac R., CSA, 46, 47
Trumpler, Charles W. A., 180, 181
Tullahoma, Tenn., 57, 101, 200
Tunstall's Station, Va., 19, 20, 23, 126
Tuscaloosa, Ala., 205

Valdeverde, N. M., 37
Valladigham, Clement. L., 94, 96
Van Dorn, Gen. Earl, CSA, 56, 86
Vicksburg, Miss., 56, 85, 86, 95, 109
Vienna, Ind., 99
Virginia, 41, 49, 57, 59, 60, 78, 127, 167, 173, 205, 212

Warden, David A., 180, 181
Warrenton, Va., 42, 58, 66
Warrenton Junction, Va., 67
Wartrace, Tenn., 112
Washington, Ga., 185, 214
Washington, D. C., 14, 39, 44, 49, 58, 64, 66, 89, 92, 97, 119, 120, 127, 167, 168, 177, 213, 215
Webb's Station, Tenn., 55
Weitzel, Gen. Godfrey, USA, 161
West, Capt. James S., CSA, 2
West Point, N. Y., 88

West, Col. Robt. M., USA, 161, 162, 163
West Virginia, 73, 167
Wheeler, Gen. Joseph, CSA, 39, 55, 108, 109, 110, 111, 112, 114, 115, 201, 203, 204, 205, 212, 213, 214, 215
White, Col. E. V., CSA, 59, 60
White House, Va., 19, 21, 23, 24, 26, 126, 142, 144, 147, 150, 152
White House, Washington, D. C., 4
Whiteside, Tenn., 116
Whiting, Capt. Charles, USA, 23
Whittaker, Capt. E. W., USA, 191
Whittaker, Capt. W. W., USA, 160
Wickham, Col. W. C., CSA, 44, 137, 149
Wilderness, Va., 134, 157
Willards Hotel, Washington, D. C., 122
Willcox, Gen. O. B., USA, 99
Willcox Landing, Va., 153
Williamsburg, Va., 77
Williamsport, Md., 51
Wilmington, N. C., 207
Wilson, Gen. James, USA, 3, 134, 141, 144, 147, 149, 155, 156, 157, 158, 159, 160, 161, 162, 163, 164, 165, 201
Wilson's Creek, Mo., 34, 104, 170, 202, 205
Winchester, Va., 8, 9, 177, 180, 181, 182, 183
Woods, Gen. William, USA, 74
Woodstock, Va., 172
Wyeth, John, CSA, 33
Wyndham, Col. Percy, USA, 64, 65, 66
Wynkoop, Col. John E., USA, 10

Yellow Tavern, Va., 137, 185
Yorktown, Va., 78
York River, Va., 19
Yorkville, S. C., 214
Young, Gen. P. M. B., CSA, 123, 124
Younger, Cole, CSA, 105